The Hands
of War

The Hands
of War

A Tale of Endurance and Hope, from a
Survivor of the Holocaust

Marione Ingram

Skyhorse Publishing

Skyhorse Publishing books may be purchased in bulk at special
discounts for sales promotion, corporate gifts, fund-raising, or educational purposes.
Special editions can also be created to specifications. For details, contact the Special Sales
Department, Skyhorse Publishing, 307 West 36th Street, 11th Floor, New York, NY 10018
or info@skyhorsepublishing.com.

Skyhorse® and Skyhorse Publishing® are registered trademarks of Skyhorse Publishing, Inc.®,
a Delaware corporation.

Visit our website at www.skyhorsepublishing.com.

Photographs are from the author's personal collection unless otherwise indicated.

"Gomorrah" first appeared in slightly different form in *Granta* (issue 96, 2006) edited by Ian Jack, and *The Best American Essays 2007*, edited by David Foster Wallace and Robert Atwan.

10 9 8 7 6 5 4 3 2 1

Library of Congress Cataloging-in-Publication Data
Ingram, Marione, author.
  The hands of war : a tale of endurance and hope, from a survivor of the Holocaust / Marione Ingram.
    volume ; cm
  Summary: "During World War II, Marione and her family miraculously escape the firestorms of Hamburg and seek shelter with a contact in the countryside who grudgingly agrees to house them in a shed for more than a year. "--Provided by publisher.
  ISBN 978-1-62087-185-0 (hardcover : alk. paper)
  1. Ingram, Marione. 2. Jews--Germany--Biography. 3. Holocaust, Jewish (1939-1945)--Germany--Personal narratives. 4. Holocaust survivors--Biography. 5. Germany--Ethnic relations. I. Title.
  DS134.42.I54A3 2013
  940.53'18092--dc23
  [B]
                         2012033052

Printed in China

For those we loved and lost,
and for Sam and Noah

A curse shall light upon the limbs of men . . .
Blood and destruction shall be so in use
And dreadful objects so familiar
That mothers shall but smile when they behold
Their infants quarter'd with the hands of war

—*Julius Caesar*, Act III, scene 1, by William Shakespeare

CONTENTS

Foreword

Marione Ingram is an extraordinary woman. As a survivor not only of the Holocaust but of the Hamburg firestorm, she is a rare witness to two of the most significant episodes of the Second World War.

I first read her memoir of these events one Halloween, and it struck me that this was a strangely appropriate time to do so. While all around me the neighborhood children were preparing for the sanitized horrors of the evening, I found myself immersed in something altogether darker. As a child, Marione suffered threats and insults from her neighbors, who were far removed from the playfulness of trick-or-treating. Other seven-year-olds would taunt her with the suggestion that she would soon be sent "up the chimney." The atmosphere in her native city of Hamburg eventually became so poisonous that her mother tried to commit suicide—something that Marione herself witnessed, and which still haunts her today.

She and her family were only saved from the Holocaust by sheer luck. A few days before they were due to be deported to a concentration camp, the British and American air forces began a bombing campaign that caused enough confusion for her family to slip through the Nazi net. But if this was a lucky escape, it did not seem so at the time. The bombing of Hamburg was an extremely traumatic event that turned Marione's entire neighborhood into a furnace. The tarmac in the streets melted, people burned as they fled the flames, and hurricane-force winds generated by the fire were strong enough to knock grown men off their feet and suck them into the inferno. Marione witnessed these horrors from the bottom of a bomb crater, where she and her mother took shelter from what we now know to be the worst single bombing raid of the European war, and the greatest man-made firestorm the world has ever seen.

In the confusion that followed the bombing, Marione and her family escaped. They saw out the rest of the war in hiding, living in a shack in the woods belonging to one of her father's pre-war Communist friends. The hunger, desperation, and loneliness she experienced during those two years were almost beyond description, and placed unbearable psychological strains on her family. Yet they survived. And not only survived, but since the war Marione has flourished—as an artist, a civil rights activist, a wife, a mother, and now a grandmother.

Like most survivor memoirs, this is a tapestry of vivid recollections, impressions, reconstructed memories, embellishments, and hearsay, but buried within it is a deeper truth: the experience of what it felt like to be there at the time. One must admire the fortitude that this extraordinary woman has shown, both in managing to survive these events and in having the courage to record them here for posterity. From the comfort of our twenty-first century world we can only thank God that our own children have never been called upon to exhibit the same kind of bravery.

Keith Lowe
Author of *Inferno: The Devastation of Hamburg, 1943*

PREFACE

This book is intended as a remembrance of family members and others who were killed because they resisted the Nazi regime or simply because they were Jews. To tell their stories, and those of some who survived, I have reconstructed from shards of memory scenes that I witnessed as a child in Hamburg, Germany, or heard about from parents and others who were there.

More than half a century after leaving, I returned to Hamburg and tried to retrace my flight through its streets during one night of Allied bombing that took forty thousand lives—a horror I had relived and set down during nights of near total recall in the 1950s. I also placed small stones on the nameless marker in the park where family members and thousands of fellow Jews were assembled for deportation to death camps. A cousin who is not a Jew reminded me that she had come to our apartment the day after my mother had received such a deportation order and had attempted suicide. Another relative told me that an uncle's suicide had been caused by his arrest for resistance activities in occupied France.

Although I was allowed to read but not copy my mother's official file and to dig for correcting and confirming facts at the University of Hamburg and its Institute for Jewish History, I do not pretend to offer a thoroughly researched history. Instead I have recounted my experiences as I recall them, aware that memory's imperfections are compounded by time and that controversy attends just about every aspect of the Holocaust. I have also taken the liberty of reconstructing some events I didn't see and conversations I didn't hear, mixing memory with a desire to convey at least the outlines of the speaker's personality.

In telling the story of Uri, a childhood friend orphaned by the Nazis, I took the additional liberty of retelling part of the story of five hundred Jewish women enslaved by Alfried Krupp, meticulously documented by William Manchester in his magnificent history, *The Arms of Krupp*. Unable to recall or confirm key elements of Uri's family tragedy, I portrayed his sister as the anonymous slave who turned back when three others made an escape from a Krupp compound in Essen. I included this fact-based fiction because Krupp's unspeakable treatment of Jewish women was soon pardoned by the American occupation authority, and the record of his "crimes against humanity" was suppressed in postwar Germany.

The Hands
of War

Chapter 1

A Child of War

As a tree may be forced by fire or lightning to bloom in winter, a child can be compelled to become an adult long before it is time. I was such a child, a child of war, an anonymous target in a global killing contest among great nations, and human prey in a genocidal war within that war. Unlike those with an early talent for music or mathematics, I didn't know that I was precocious, only that the imminence of violent death demanded an absolute commitment to life. In Hamburg, Germany, during the summer of 1943, it required even more.

At the center of the most devastating firestorm any war had ever spawned, the hatreds unleashed by the internal war against Jews ironically delivered me from the horrifying massacre of civilians by Allied bombers. Because my neighbors would not let me share their bomb shelter, I escaped through Hamburg's exploding streets while they were baked like loaves of bread in an oven. Some forty thousand civilians, mainly women and children, were killed that night in what was by far the deadliest bombing there had ever been. The RAF commanders who planned and directed the killing called it Operation Gomorrah. They and their American counterparts kept at it for ten nights and days, punishing the city with successive attacks, slaughtering thousands more, continuing to bomb even after there was almost no one left to kill, covering my tracks with the ashes of the dead.

By the age of eight, I already knew better than to believe in miracles or to think that the bombers had taken the lives of so many others in order to save me from the hands of war. I also understood that I was different and yet not different from those who wouldn't let me share their air-raid shelter, and that the differences they ascribed to me as a Jew were based on hateful lies. Usually I knew what was expected of me and did as I was instructed by my parents. Of course, even when I was aware that others' lives depended upon me, I couldn't behave like an adult all the time. A few days before the RAF launched Operation Gomorrah, my mother told me to take my baby sister, Rena, to Cousin Inge's apartment in another part of the city and to wait for her there. But on the way I decided to disobey my mother, and I shall be forever glad I did.

My mother, three-year-old Rena, and I were living in a walk-up apartment in Hamburg, a proudly ancient seaport that boasted the busiest shipyards and bawdiest nightlife on the continent. My father was serving in a Luftwaffe unit stationed in Belgium, and another younger sister, Helga, was living on a farm outside the city. Despite the disquieting look in Mother's eyes that day when I set out for Inge's apartment, I was thrilled to be outside, unsupervised and in charge. It had been an unusually hot and dry summer but a salt breeze from the North Sea cooled my cheeks and seemed to calm Rena as I rolled her along inside a wicker carriage with spoke wheels and a handle as high as my chin.

Our street, Hasselbrook Strasse, showed few signs of damage from the scores of air raids the city already had experienced. Angling through the Eilbeck district toward Alster Lake in the center of Hamburg, the street was lined on both sides by shade trees and apartment buildings ornamented with sinuous art nouveau designs and stone faces that were much friendlier than the real ones I usually

Holding Mother's hands before the bombings began.

encountered in the city's streets. After pushing the pram for about ten blocks, I hesitated at a small park where a wooden sign decreed that the sandbox, teeter-totter and swings were "For Aryans Only." After sticking out my tongue at the sign, I climbed onto a swing and began kicking my feet toward clouds that were strung like bed sheets across the steepled sky.

Despite the delicious feel of the breeze under my skirt I couldn't shake off the feeling that something had gone seriously wrong at home. Mother had cried most of the night and wouldn't tell me why. I had never been sent on my own to Cousin Inge's or been entrusted to take Rena so far from home. Although I had solemnly promised to go straight away to Inge's apartment without so much as a backward glance, I couldn't make myself continue. I climbed down from the swing and pointed the carriage back toward home. Hurrying past the bakery shop where I had once enjoyed strawberry and lemon ice cream in a crunchy pastry shell, I didn't slow down until I reached our apartment building.

Without removing my sister, I parked the carriage in the stairwell and bounded noiselessly up five flights to our apartment on the top floor. When the door wouldn't open and there was no response to my knocking and calling out, I thought with relief that Mother must have locked up and was on her way to Inge's. But when I pushed harder with my shoulder the door suddenly yielded and I almost fell inside. Looking about I saw Mother slumped on the floor in front of the kitchen stove.

For a moment I just stood there, listening to the gas jets hiss like angry geese. Because she had a six-pointed yellow star on her dress, there was no one I could call upon for help. It hadn't always been that way, but it was now late July in 1943, and those who might have helped in the past had long since been silenced.

"Wake up, Mother!" I pleaded repeatedly, shaking her and slapping her cheek. I even attempted to imitate my father by calling her by her first name. "Wake up, Margarete! Margarete, wake up!"

Trying not to inhale too much of the gas, I pulled Mother away from the stove, tugging first one limp arm and then the other. I managed to get her head and a shoulder into the dining room, but there her clothes bunched and clung to the carpet. So I took down the blackout drape that covered the dining-room window, swung back the glass pane and welcomed the air into the room and into my lungs. Mother was lying partially on one side but mainly on her back, with her eyes shut and her lips slightly parted. She was very pale and completely limp and I couldn't tell for certain whether she was breathing. But I believed she was still alive.

At times I thought I could detect a slight movement in her chest, but the longer I stared the more uncertain I became. Putting my ear there was equally maddening. Just when I felt sure that I could hear a faint heartbeat, a rustle of cloth or some other noise would smother the sound. As I sat on the floor with Mother's head in my lap, unsure of what to do next, I began to hear the faint sound of my baby sister crying in the stairwell below. Worrying that Mother might be cross with me for abandoning Rena, I slipped out from under her head and hurried down the stairs to fetch my sister.

While I was carrying Rena up the stairs, I was tempted to stop on the third floor and ask Frau Wiederman for help. Once she had been friendly and I had played with her daughter, Monika, who had adored holding my beautiful Kate Kruse doll. But after Herr Wiederman joined the Nazi Party and was made block warden, his wife had become the most vocal enforcer of the "Aryans-Only" rules, and Monika had wrinkled her nose, pursed her lips and declared, "I don't play with Jew pigs!" So I kept climbing, believing they would more likely harm than help us.

Mother was just as I had left her. I placed Rena on the floor beside her, hoping that my sister's cries of hunger would somehow awaken her. They didn't. So I put a pillow under Mother's head and began to look around for something that Rena and I could eat. I found a few potatoes, washed them and put them in a pot with water. Then

I scratched a match and tried to light the stove, which caused a frightening flash and a loud pop followed by the smell of my singed hair. I tried again and again, until the gas ring finally produced a steady flame. When they were cooked, I mashed the potatoes and fed them to Rena. Afterwards, I changed her and put her on the bed where all three of us slept when Father was away.

I wished that my father had been stationed in Hamburg instead of in Brussels. Because he was not a Jew but a uniformed member of Reichsminister Goering's procurement command, and was also the most resourceful person anybody knew, I felt certain that he would have been able to save her. He'd been recruited for the Luftwaffe by a group of Storm Troopers who had beaten him almost to death—permanently injuring his kidneys—and given him the choice of joining up or dying together with his Jewish wife and children. Although his unit helped to keep Germans relatively well fed at the expense of the occupied peoples, he used his position to supply the top brass with fine cognac and other wartime luxuries and even to arrange for certain officers to have their portrait painted by a noted artist, his friend, Herman Koeller. Gaining first the confidence and then the secrets of these high-ranking officials, Father would then pass on information to contacts in the Resistance, many of whom were former comrades from his communist youth or people he knew from his prewar import-export business.

My thoughts turned next to my middle sister, Helga, with whose help, I thought, we would at least be able to move Mother onto the bed. Helga had been fortunate enough to inherit Father's coloring— he was from the North Sea coastal area of Friesland, and like many of the people there had Viking blood in his veins. Helga's light blond hair, blue-green eyes and pale skin were her Aryan passport, enabling Father to place her with a family that lived on a farm on the outskirts of Hamburg. There she was accepted without question as one more child from the city who was farmed out with relatives to escape the bombing raids.

My father, Edward Emil Oestreicher in 1939.

Before putting up the blackout drapes and shutting out the last of the light, I looked around the apartment, hoping to see something—I didn't know what—that would help me to understand what had happened. Although I was a capable reader, Mother hadn't left a note that would explain why she had decided to take her own life. But there was a photo album on the dining table which had been removed from its normal place in the living room. A few pictures had been taken out and left on the table, and the album was open to a group picture taken at a double wedding that must have been quite a fabulous occasion.

The brides were seated in clouds of white tulle between their grooms, surrounded by some fifty people standing or seated and looking at the camera. The brides' smiles were restrained but I could tell that they were very happy, while the grooms looked rather pensive. Mother was seated on the floor in front of one of the grooms, looking up wistfully, smiling but with a faint suggestion of tears that I hadn't noticed before. I had seen the photo many times and knew that Mother had been about ten or eleven at the time, that almost everyone in the photo was related to her and that she was the only one still living in Germany who hadn't been taken by the Nazis.

I picked up a picture of Grandfather Siegfried Singer and thought he looked sad. It made me feel strange to realize that Mother may have been looking at his photo while I was outside swinging. For reasons that had never been fully explained to me, my grandfather had killed himself before I was born, leaving behind his wife Rosa, my mother, his son Hans, his sister Emma and other relatives. I shuddered at the thought that Grandfather's example might have inspired Mother's behavior. More likely she had been overcome with grief thinking about her mother, her brother, and her aunt. It had been a year and a half since the three of them had been deported to Minsk in occupied Russia along with some fifteen hundred other Hamburg Jews. Although there had been no word from them since, and she had been told that the deportees had been killed, Mother

Mother, aged ten, sits below right of brides at family double wedding in 1922.

had refused to give up hope. If she had just now received some confirmation of their deaths, I reasoned, that might explain her attempt to kill herself, but I saw no sign of this among the photos strewn across the table.

As I put a photo of Grandmother back into the album, I looked to see if she was wearing her teardrop pearl earrings. I didn't see them there but her warmth, her spirited way of doing things, even the lily-of-the-valley scent of her powder came back to me. She had lived with my uncle, Hans, only a few blocks from us on Hasselbrook Strasse. Ten days before the police came for Grandmother, Hans and Aunt Emma had been ordered to report to Moorweide Park for deportation. The park was on the other side of Alster Lake, next to the Hamburg University Library and across the street from one of the two large train stations in the downtown area. Countless numbers of Hamburgers, including me, had watched as Hans and Emma and almost a thousand other deportees had walked baggage in hand across the city to the park. Before being herded into boxcars they remained in the park for many hours, an encamped spectacle surrounded by armed guards and police dogs with gleaming eyes. Although there were not nearly as many spectators as had jammed the streets in earlier days to cheer their Fuehrer, everyone in the city was made aware that on this day the Nazis had made good on his promise to get rid of Jews.

So when Grandmother received her order to report to Moorweide Park, she refused to go. Although she asked us to leave, Mother and I waited with her in her apartment for the police to arrive. We knew, because she had told us more than once, that her heart had been broken when socialist firebrand, Rosa Luxemburg, had been murdered by the police and broken again when her husband had died. But the deportations of Hans and Aunt Emma had put her in a cold fury. Seeing our deep anxiety, she told us we shouldn't worry about her, that she would probably be sent to the place where Hans and Emma had been taken and that she would be glad to be reunited with them even if the conditions were harsh. Although she would

Grandmother Rosa Wolff Singer, deported and murdered in November 1941

Great Aunt Emma, deported and murdered in November 1941

not cooperate with the Nazis, she instructed us to remain calm and try not to interfere with the police.

When the police arrived Grandmother told them that she would go with them only if they returned her son. An officer wearing a black SS uniform told her that she would soon be reunited with Hans and ordered two soldiers to pick her up and put her in a van parked outside. Streaming tears, Mother pleaded with the authorities to wait until she could finish putting a few things into a bag for Grandmother to take with her. I was clinging to Grandmother, who quietly stroked my head in an attempt to calm me. When the two soldiers approached, I attacked the nearest one with my fists, but Grandmother pulled me back. Before she was lifted into the van, she quickly removed her pearl earrings and gave them to me, kissed me, and wished me a happy birthday. A soldier grabbed my wrist and tried to force me to give up the earrings, but the SS officer ordered him to let me go. "It's her *birthday*!" he said sardonically.

"Tomorrow," I said, angrily correcting him. "*Tomorrow* is my birthday!"

* * *

Word trickled back to the city that those who had been deported to Minsk had been killed soon after. Mother wouldn't believe that this had happened to all of the deportees. We knew several people who had been sent to other camps and were still alive after months of incarceration. We hoped and even imagined that Grandmother, Hans, and Emma had somehow managed to be reunited. Mother begged for news of them on the days when she was required to report to the Gestapo on her activities during the preceding week. I hated those occasions even more than the air raids and worried about her from the moment she left until her return, sometimes hours later. On one of those grim visits she was told that her relatives had been killed upon arrival at Minsk. She refused to believe him but told herself that the Gestapo official was lying to break her will. Another time she was told that Grandmother had not been sent to Minsk with the others, because the van the soldiers had put her into was itself a travelling death chamber.

Mother told me that Grandmother had tried to get Hans to go to the United States before the war started. Although the Americans had turned down most Jews who wanted to leave, Grandmother had lived in New York for two years when she and Grandfather were first married. In fact they had been married there. With the help of American friends she had managed to get permission to emigrate with Hans, who was then seventeen. But Hans couldn't be persuaded to leave Hamburg, because he was in love and the girl hadn't been able to get a visa for America. Both Hans and his beloved were later deported to Minsk on the same train.

Mother had not been the same after those deportations. Remembering her transformation made my eyes moist and I tried to recall earlier, better times. I remembered that Hans had taught me to read, starting when I was about four. This was one of the happiest experiences I could imagine and looking at his picture I could almost hear his soft voice whispering the name of a word if I didn't recall it. Aunt Emma also had given me good memories. She lived near Inge in the St. George district, and when she visited she would pinch my cheek and tell me to be proud that I was a Singer because the Singers had been chamberlains to the Czars.

After closing and putting away the photo album, I looked in the small box where I kept Grandmother's earrings to see if they were still there. They were. Beside the box was a licorice mask shaped like Winston Churchill, complete with a licorice cigar. Father had brought it on his last visit, promising that the cheeky Prime Minister, whose face adorned dart boards in Hamburg pubs, was coming to our rescue. I treasured the mask, sometimes licked it and frequently talked to it, especially during air raids. But there hadn't been one recently and the mask looked a bit dusty. I gave it a lick anyway. Then I decided that, since I couldn't put Mother on the bed, I would put Rena beside her and the three of us would spend the night on the floor. Although there was no air raid that night, I lay awake for long stretches, listening for Mother's every breath and watching to see if she opened her eyes.

I couldn't let myself believe that she wouldn't awaken, but I wasn't sure what I would do if she was still asleep in the morning. Thinking hard about our situation and trying to come up with the reason Mother had decided to take her own life, I realized that she probably had suffered much more than she had allowed me to see, and I had seen plenty of hurtful things as she battled the Gestapo and other officials and even our neighbors. I had noticed that she looked more tired and subdued since the deportations, but I was more impressed by how brave and defiant she was, how smart she looked whenever she left the apartment, and how confidently she walked through streets choked with armed men in uniform and prisoners in striped clothing. At home she didn't mope about or cry and complain; instead, she kept us both busy doing chores or reading or plotting how to get around the ever increasing restrictions on Jews. When I felt bored or blue, she would sometimes sing to me, usually Schubert lieder or songs from operettas or even arias from grand opera. I not only loved her, I admired her and wanted more than anything else to be like her.

On his last visit, Father had been cheerful and brisk as usual when he first arrived. He called Mother his valiant "Garde Offizier," and pulled presents—mostly food—out of his bag with the flare of a magician producing a live pet. He kissed Rena, held her over his head until she began to protest, and then presented her with a small stuffed bear with a blue ribbon around its neck. She examined it all over before thanking him with a smile. He smiled back and rummaged in his bag again, then slowly withdrew a beautiful, new brown leather book bag with leather straps which he slipped over my shoulders and deftly adjusted. This was what Aryan children from affluent families wore to school—the rest wore bags made of canvas or a similarly tough fabric—and was what I envied them for the most, even more than the fact that they could go to school and I couldn't. Father said it was made of Belgian leather, the same as his winter overcoat, and I was sure it was finer than the best German book bags, including those worn by arrogant Hitler Youths. Inhaling the rich aroma, I opened its flap and almost choked up with pleasure. Inside it were two schoolbooks, paper, some of it plain and the rest lined, a pencil box with pencils, an eraser, and a box of watercolors. After I thanked him, hugging him with all my might, I also found a pair of blunt scissors in the small leather pocket on the outside of the bag. I showed it all to Mother, who knew how often I had wished for school materials, and immediately set about drawing, coloring and cutting out images of children, adults, plants, and animals that I hoped, when assembled, would convey some of the deep satisfaction I felt.

I worked diligently but listened attentively as Mother and Father quietly discussed our current situation, which had deteriorated considerably since his last visit. I didn't have to overhear to know that our circumstance had grown dramatically more threatened, not so much by Allied bombers, which had already attacked Hamburg more than a hundred times and likely would come again, but by the authorities, which were closing in on Jews who were married to Gentiles. Such marriages had been forbidden not long after I was born, but existing marriages had been excused from complying with some of the hundreds of laws and regulations designed to isolate, immobilize, and depopulate Jewish communities. This was why we hadn't been forced to move into the designated Jewish quarter, why we had been issued special cards that enabled us to buy some rationed foods, and why until recently we had not been required to wear the yellow star. Though I never heard Mother or Father say so, I understood that their marriage and the fact that Father was in the Luftwaffe were the main reasons we hadn't been deported along with Grandmother and Hans and Aunt Emma or any of the Jews sent

"Let Father see what you're reading." (My mother's comment on
the back of this 1940 photo.)

away since then. But listening to them as I drew and cut out paper images, I learned that other Jewish men and women had recently been deported despite being married to a Gentile. Mother looked saddened and tired and somewhat skeptical as Father reassured her that he was working on some of his former communist comrades, including the couple who were sheltering my middle sister, Helga, to help us go into hiding.

Father was a wellspring of inside information on developments in the wars that raged outside our apartment. Other adults, including some of his brothers, used to come to our apartment seeking his advice on how to deal with the Nazis, and in Mother's view he was much too reckless in sharing information obtained through his obsessive efforts to subvert the regime. Although I didn't always understand everything that was said, I had been an avid listener on such occasions. By the time of this visit, we seldom had any guests, but he had always been my personal tutor on how to stand up to the Nazis without giving them grounds for arresting one of us. Although I already knew how to comport myself, he sat me down for a serious talk before he went back to his Luftwaffe unit. He reminded me that he counted on me to look after Rena whenever Mother was away. He told me yet again to stay close to Mother, to follow her lead, and to do as she said without hesitation. But this time he added that I should look for ways to lighten her burden and help her out at all times.

"I promised your grandmother that I would take care of her," he said, "and I need you to help me keep that promise when I'm away."

Several days after he had gone back to his Luftwaffe unit, I noticed that Mother looked unhappy, and I remembered what he had said. So I asked her if she was feeling all right and if there was anything I could do to help. She smiled and said she was fine, adding that I could change Rena's dress. It was obvious that the smile was forced, but I could not get her to talk to me about the things that had made her so unhappy. She couldn't answer any of my questions about her family, then or ever after, without dissolving in tears. The loss of her loved ones had been too painful, and I had been with her when they were taken by the Nazis. Except for what I had experienced with them or heard others say about them, most of what I came to know about Mother's parents I learned from my father after the war, when he tried to get the German government to compensate Mother for valuable books, including a Shakespeare first folio her parents had acquired in America when they were living there "in exile" at the beginning of the twentieth century.

My younger sister Helga and I plot mischief before the war.

Chapter 2

Mother's Story

Ten years before she tried to take her own life, my mother, whose maiden name was Margarete Singer, had shocked her mother by confiding that she wanted to marry Erhard Ernst Emil Oestreicher, who was known as Eddie and was neither a Jew nor a practicing Christian, but a communist with deep-set sea-blue eyes and dark golden hair flowing back from a broad forehead. Eddie's mother, who had lost two husbands and raised seven sons and two daughters in Friesland, the wind-swept North Sea area shared by Holland and Germany, made no objection to his marriage plans. And Margarete's mother, Rosa Wolff Singer, soon softened her opposition to the "mixed marriage," after being reminded of the furor she had created with her own spectacularly disobedient elopement with my grandfather, Siegfried Singer, shortly after the turn of the century.

Siegfried was the scion of a wealthy orthodox family that had fled St. Petersburg one bribe in front of the secret police of Czar Alexander II, who had freed the serfs but jailed Jewish intellectuals because he believed—not entirely without cause—that they were plotting revolution. Growing up in Hamburg, Siegfried matured as a scholarly, somewhat reserved young man with unconventional ideas and an antiquated Roman sense of honor. To his parents' consternation, however, he was intrigued by socialist politics and Rosa Wolff, a well-read young political activist who made hats for a department store.

Siegfried and Rosa met at a Socialists' rally on a dripping day in mid-December, 1900, in Hamburg's militantly working-class district of Winterhude. He was charmed by the cheerfully assertive manner in which she presented a small bouquet of red roses to the main speaker, Rosa Luxemburg, upon the latter's arrival at the cavernous tavern on Muhlenkamp Strasse where the rally was being held. Like many of the onlookers he noticed a resemblance between the two women and wondered if they were related. He also was intrigued by the younger Rosa's command of her petite hourglass figure, which contrasted with his own tall, rectilinear body, prominently topped by a square-cut, prematurely dignified head.

After Rosa Luxemburg disappeared inside the teeming tavern to take a place on a raised boxing-ring platform, the younger Rosa remained outside, handing out leaflets that called for the support of seamstresses who had lost their livelihood for daring to complain about sweatshop conditions. Siegfried took one of the leaflets and carefully read it through despite the persistent rain that made steam rise from police horses and caused both riders and mounts to snort impatiently.

Inside the tavern, Rosa Luxemburg spoke through a large megaphone, silencing the boisterous hubbub with carefully reasoned appeals for international worker solidarity. Many in the crowd applauded her scornful depiction of businessmen who grew fat by paying starvation wages, and some grunted in agreement when she told them that the coal miners then on strike in Poland were fighting for workers everywhere. Their sinews and sphincters tightened, however, when she aimed her lance at worker apathy, insisting that the working man or woman who refused to stand with his or her brothers or sisters was stealing desperately needed food from other workers' families. As she paused to let the point sink

Socialist firebrand Rosa Luxemburg was killed in 1919 while in police custody. Here she is (right) with Clara Zetkin in 1910 on her way to the Social Democratic Party Congress.

deeper, there was a low grumbling and much shuffling of feet. And when she put down the megaphone and stepped back, hundreds of workers shook their fists or raised their mugs and roared their approval of what she had just said.

Noticing that several dozen brawny men with rocks and sticks— hired thugs from Hamburg's Eppendorf and Barmbeck districts— had joined the policemen near the entrance to the bar, Siegfried tried to persuade Rosa Wolff to leave the area. But she pretended to be as indifferent to the threat posed by the newcomers as she was to the rain. A few minutes later the bar began to erupt workers who, forgetting all about international brotherhood, took violent exception to the hostile attitudes of the ruffians and their police escort. Without waiting Siegfried wrapped the flap of his coat like a great sheltering wing around the diminutive Rosa and guided her through the bruising melee to the sanctuary of an unlicensed tavern two blocks away on Gertigstrasse. Space was made for them on adjoining benches in a dark corner and a lit candle was welded by its own tallow to the table in front of them. Someone fed a couple of lengths of split oak into a nearby tile stove. Rosa removed the pins from her hair, letting it fall about her shoulders so that it could dry more easily. Siegfried and Rosa both ordered cabbage soup and roasted potatoes topped by fried eggs, accompanying both courses with slowly drawn pints of local lager.

Although the bar was gregariously boisterous, Siegfried and Rosa quietly discussed politics and literature and each took the measure of the other's knowledge of Talmudic and other philosophies. After homemade schnapps, courtesy of the owner, a large man with a serious mustache, they began to laugh about the paradoxical absurdities of Jewish life in Hamburg. When they could laugh no more, they argued. Siegfried agreed that the large department stores were shameful in their treatment of the women who made their clothes and hats, but he challenged Rosa's belief that Jewish ownership of the store compounded the offense. After debating utopian versus revolutionary socialism, they agreed that every prescription for violence was inherently repugnant and that bomb-throwing anarchists undermined rather than advanced social justice. They also agreed that class warfare was inevitable, but concluded on a cheerful note as she promised to sponsor his membership in the wonderful consumer cooperative only a block or two from where they were sitting.

By the time Rosa and Siegfried had completed the long walk to her home, each was convinced the other was the smartest young person of the opposite sex either had ever met. Despite the cold they talked for another half-hour at the entrance to her apartment building. Although Siegfried normally deliberated for days or sometimes for weeks before reaching an important decision, he made up his mind within minutes of leaving Rosa that he would propose to her before the New Year began.

Despite their reputation for ignoring class distinctions, Siegfried's parents were terribly upset when they learned he intended to marry Rosa Wolff. It wasn't that they personally disliked her or disapproved of her political activism. But in this prosperous, cosmopolitan seaport, where successful Jews not only were emancipated but also assimilated to a degree unimagined in Russia, they had groomed their gifted son to marry one of the several Jewish merchant princesses.

In addition to a superb German education Siegfried had been given a year of study in London, the favorite "other" city of Hamburg's elite. His parents also had purchased a controlling interest in a thriving boot factory, anticipating the day when practical considerations would temper their son's passion for literature and philosophy. Their solution to the problem of the petite milliner with soft eyes and a sharp mind was to exile Siegfried to America to learn the secrets of mass marketing. If Siegfried and Rosa still wanted to wed after a two-year separation, they could do so in Hamburg with his parents' blessing.

My mother's parents, Rosa and Siegfried Singer.

New York City at the beginning of the twentieth century was not a place to dampen Siegfried's passion. Within a month he purchased Rosa's passage on the *Deutschland*, a Hamburg-built liner that held the record for the fastest Atlantic crossing: five days, seven hours and thirty-eight minutes from Plymouth, England, to New York. They were wed shortly after she arrived in New York and lived in lower Manhattan for the next two years. Siegfried made an effort to learn about business, but mostly they savored the city's cultural smorgasbord and collected books in several languages.

Siegfried's love affair with the works of Shakespeare, which had begun during his year of study in London, was consummated in New York by the acquisition of a Shakespeare First Folio. At the time there were only two such First Folios in America. Siegfried and Rosa's treasure was purchased through one of New York's most prominent publishing firms. After they returned to Hamburg, to live in a seven-room apartment on Rosenstrasse, the First Folio was the centerpiece of their collection of rare books, which attracted scholars from yeshivas and universities across Europe both before and after the war that began in 1914.

Although he had a two-year-old daughter and a factory that was an important source of boots for the military, Siegfried volunteered for the Wehrmacht, as did thousands of Jews who might have avoided military service but who wanted to demonstrate their patriotism. Fluent in English and Russian, he was often assigned to regimental headquarters to interrogate prisoners of war. Occasionally, he surprised a captured Londoner or New Yorker with his knowledge of their city. He also surprised fellow officers by his ability to quote extended passages from the works of Nietzche.

The regimental Junkers' severe disdain for the Jewish intellectual who was named after a favorite hero of Aryan mythology was replaced by respect after British tanks shredded German lines in September 1918. While others prepared to surrender the overrun command post, Siegfried organized lightly armed clerks and runners

My mother at approximately two years old.

to hold off the Tommies long enough for senior officers to withdraw to a new position in Belgium. He then led the surviving remnant through British lines, using darkness and his command of upper-class English to convince sentries that he was shepherding prisoners to an internment pen.

Siegfried was recuperating from influenza at a hospital in Belgium when the ringing of church bells signaled the armistice on November 11, 1918. While the local people were overjoyed, Siegfried's comrades were stunned by the news that Kaiser Wilhelm had fled to exile in Holland and a republic had been declared at home. Since the German army was still firmly entrenched on foreign soil and confident of its ability to defend the Fatherland, many felt terribly betrayed. But Siegfried told everyone near him that America's entry into the war had tilted the balance of power so drastically that continued fighting was futile. He insisted that the High Command's greatest blunder had been to order U-boats to sink American passenger ships, and he urged anyone who would listen to be thankful it had been stopped before the homeland became the battleground.

* * *

During Siegfried's recuperation, his wife, Rosa, was engaged in a tumultuous political battle that threatened to become bloody. A week before the Armistice, Hamburg was thrown into a frenzy of fractured loyalties when sailors there and in other northern ports mutinied rather than obeyed orders to take the offensive against the more powerful Allied fleet. Sensing the prospect of real power, the Socialist Party split into factions that attacked one another more zealously than they opposed the tottering monarchy. Rosa was in the streets and at countless worker-soldier council meetings, urging socialist unity, the tabling of disputes over power sharing, and concerted pressure to end the war.

When a panicked prince dethroned the Kaiser by announcing an abdication that hadn't occurred but couldn't be effectively retracted, the Socialists quickly proclaimed a republic and took over the government. The new leadership included various socialist factions and even ministers from the deposed imperial regime. But it excluded Rosa Luxemburg and her more radical Spartacist faction.

Rosa Singer agreed with the more moderate approach of the center party, which was willing to accept piecemeal socialist reforms to gain wider support for the new republic. She feared that the Spartacists' prescription for a complete break with the politics and economics of the past would provoke civil war at home and prolong the fighting with England, France, and America. But when Rosa Luxemburg was arrested and brutally murdered in police custody, Rosa Singer felt as if a truncheon had struck her own breastbone. Although she didn't alter her principles, Rosa Singer's faith in the future had been destroyed, and the loss was subtly but permanently etched in her expression.

Although the postwar years were less deadly, Siegfried and Rosa felt they were in some ways more deranged. Reparations exacted by the war's European victors fueled runaway inflation that pushed the price of a postage stamp to fifty billion Deutchmarks. As hunger and poverty became more widespread, unemployed shipyard and factory workers took to the streets with destitute former soldiers and sailors in a desperate effort to establish a Marxist regime in Hamburg. After bloody pitched battles, regular army units put down the uprisings and shot or imprisoned the leaders. In the regional governments to the south, right-wing paramilitary groups, also claiming to represent jobless workers, tried repeatedly to bludgeon and bluff their way into power.

In time Siegfried and Rosa agreed that the perverted mythology of the Nazis, rather than the polemics of Lenin or Trotsky, was the pottage for which Germans would trade their undervalued republic. Street-corner Storm Troopers handed out leaflets claiming that Germany had not been defeated on the battlefield but had been sold out and served up by Jews. These "November traitors" also had reaped enormous profits by overcharging for war materials, the troopers declared. Like spores from noxious mushrooms, Nazi propaganda seeded itself in the common misery and the conviction that Aryans had a superior culture and were better educated, harder working and more disciplined than everyone else. Even after their bungled "beer-hall putsch" landed many of their leaders in jail and made them the butt of countless jokes, the Nazis continued to attract support.

Despite all the angst and near anarchy, however, five years after signing the Treaty of Versailles the ugly-duckling republic began to develop a long white neck. Soon beer halls that had reverberated to the ranting of brown shirts were bustling with tourists from countries that until recently had been despised enemies. Rhine steamers, Black Forest trails, taverns and ratskellers hosted countless brief encounters in foreign tongues. While Paris continued to mesmerize American expatriates, Berlin became the city of choice for sojourners who wanted to experience the sensation of living "beyond good and evil."

Regardless of his preference for books over boots, Siegfried shared in the burgeoning prosperity. He and Rosa frequented the Hamburg Opera, concert halls, galleries, and other cultural institutions and added rare books and precious works of Hebrew theology and philosophy to their library. They were on the boards or were members of various charitable associations and cultural societies, both Jewish and secular, and made their home a haven for serious discourse.

For her seventeenth birthday daughter Margarete was given a season in Paris, which her mother viewed as a practical finishing school for a somewhat sheltered young woman who would soon be making life-shaping choices. Remembering her own utter bewilderment upon entering the cultural carnival of fin de siècle New York, Rosa wanted to ensure that her daughter's choices were as informed and assured as possible. Where better than Paris, the city of light, with its matchless commitment to esthetic, intellectual, and material refinements, for her daughter to develop the confidence

Hans, who was born nine years after my mother, and his nanny.

Mother holding her brother, Hans, in 1922.

My Uncle Hans, circa 1924, who was later deported and murdered in 1941.

to deal gracefully with a world that could be extraordinarily kind one moment and unbelievably cruel the next?

Rosa believed that it would also be good for her son, Hans, to have his father's undivided attention for a time, and good for Siegfried to have Hans's companionship. Handsome, bright and able to please without effort, Hans seemed to be everyone's favorite younger brother. Despite the disparity in ages, Margarete's friends adored him almost as much as she did. But Rosa felt there was a too-polite distance between father and son. She knew that Siegfried bitterly regretted letting his autocratic father saddle him with the boot factory. Running a business not only didn't suit Siegfried, it frequently depressed him for days on end. When a friend went out of business after losing key contracts and credit, Siegfried was more upset than the injured party. He believed that competitors had ruined his friend by exploiting anti-Jewish attitudes.

Rosa and Margarete arrived in Paris in mid-October, when chestnuts were falling and cracking their horny shells on the roofs of taxis. They sent their trunks ahead by cab and went by open carriage from the train station to The Ritz. Still a believer in democratic socialism, Rosa nevertheless wished Margarete to experience service fit for nobility. Her own household, Rosa knew, was too informal to serve as a model for a young woman who might marry into a family in which ritual formality was observed every day and not merely when guests were invited.

Margarete's season in Paris was undermined, however, by the crashing of financial markets, first in the New World and then the Old. Perhaps because the crimson plush at the Ritz effectively absorbed external shocks, Rosa at first underestimated the severity of the downturn. As the autumn progressed and the wind stripped the trees, there were noticeably fewer tables set in the Ritz dining room. But this seemed no more surprising than the inevitable whisperings that Jews were to blame for the crisis. Siegfried's letters made no mention of a drastic drop in sales but spoke only of golden

My mother (right) with her younger brother, Hans, seated directly in front of their parents.

moments with Hans, which greatly pleased Rosa. Since Margarete had met some attractive young internationals, neither mother nor daughter was in a hurry to return to Hamburg.

Their idyll ended abruptly, however, when Hans wrote Margarete that Siegfried was discouraged by the new wave of anti-Semitism fueled by the financial slump. Hans said that Siegfried was still despondent over the bankruptcy of his friend and that he believed the problem was getting insurmountable. Instead of doing things together, Hans said, Siegfried spent hours alone in his study writing articles that were never published, in response to anti-Jewish screeds.

On the train to Hamburg, Rosa smiled at Margarete's excitement at the prospect of being reunited with her brother and her father, but couldn't escape the feeling that she had stayed too long in Paris. When there was no one to greet them at the station, Rosa arranged for one taxi to take her home immediately and another to follow with Margarete and the luggage.

Rosa arrived at their apartment on Rosenstrasse to a scene of utter desolation. An hour earlier Siegfried had put on his dress uniform, locked himself in his study, taken his service revolver from a locked drawer and shot himself through the heart. The servants, hearing the shot and being unable to enter the study, had phoned the police and summoned a doctor and an ambulance. Before they arrived, however, Hans and a servant had succeeded in breaking open the heavy wooden door. When Rosa entered the room Hans was still lying on the floor embracing his father's bloodstained chest. A handwritten note apologizing to Rosa and the family was on the desk. Siegfried gave no explanation for his action, but his family and those who knew him well attributed it to despair over the attacks on Jews, rather than to a fear of business failure.

* * *

It was three years later that Emma Singer Muller, Siegfried's tall and more robust younger sister, attempted to reawaken Margarete's interest in young men. Emma believed that women should be entitled to equal rights with men and, moreover, that it made no difference whether the woman was single or married. Witty and worldly, Emma had waited until she was almost thirty to marry, because, as she said, "it was so much fun being single." After marrying, she saw no good reason why she should stop having fun. Rather than children she first chose to have a second apartment in Paris. Even after her husband sold the apartment to keep the French from confiscating it during The Great War, and after she gave birth to a son, Kurt, she continued to visit friends there almost every year.

Having known and loved Siegfried longer than Rosa, Emma had little patience for Rosa's feelings of guilt about his death. Emma respected and loved her sister-in-law, but vociferously opposed the notion that Rosa could have saved Siegfried from himself. She insisted that her brother had always done exactly as he chose, that he didn't tell others what to do and wouldn't ask anyone for help. Even though she had been in Hamburg while Rosa was away and had seen him often, he had given no indication that he was unusually depressed but, on the contrary, had told her how pleased he was to have the opportunity to spend more time with Hans.

Despite the hardships of The Great Depression or, perhaps, because of them, Hamburgers were socializing as never before. Unless the weather was really foul, friends and strangers would gather to share a pot of coffee or keg of beer beside the Alster, or simply to talk or listen to an accordion. Everyone who could crawl attended street fairs, and couples of all ages privately polished dance routines to compete in immensely popular contests. Emma knew that Margarete loved to dance and she knew a very attractive young man who was an accomplished ball-room dancer. Although her friend, Eddie, also was adept at opening bedroom doors, and he was not a Jew, Emma believed that she could trust him with Margarete.

Even though she was a monarchist and he a communist, Emma appreciated Eddie for not being a conventional Hamburger who said and pretended to do whatever social norms prescribed. He was from Friesland, the North Sea area claimed by Germany and the Netherlands, but which really belongs only to itself. Although his father had died at sea, Eddie had gone to sea after finishing high school and had made the world his university. He read everything he could get his hands on and would sometimes leave a ship and stay in a foreign country until he was ready to sign on with another. After seven years, he was able to speak seven languages and knew quite a bit about the cultures that competed for prominence, commerce or merely space in the world. Along the way he acquired an abiding interest in politics and philosophy and a passion for the arts, but never lost the impish streak that amused and occasionally confounded those around him. Emma noted that other people also turned to him for unorthodox direction or, in her case, collaboration, perhaps because they sensed that whatever he undertook would have an interesting, if not a completely successful, outcome.

Emma told Eddie that her niece was as dear to her as her own son and that she was beautiful and intelligent and should be stumbling over suitors whenever she stepped out. The trouble was, she refused to step out; in fact she almost never left her mother's apartment.

Eddie pondered this for a moment and quietly asked why.

Emma explained that her brother, Margarete's father, had killed himself three years earlier and Margarete could not seem to break out of the habit of mourning.

After expressing sympathy for Emma's and Margarete's loss, Eddie asked Emma what she thought he could do to help.

Emma was ready with a scheme to reintroduce Margarete to something approaching a normal social life for a young woman in Hamburg. She told Eddie that she would somehow induce Margarete to go with her to the Alster Pavilion, where he would "happen by" and would be introduced as a "dear friend" and invited to join their table. After talking for a while and enjoying the music and a glass or two of *sekt*, Margarete might be persuaded to dance. Emma said that Margarete had loved to dance before her father's death and that dancing could be the tool to crack the shell of grief that had thickened around her. Emma made it clear that she was not interested in matchmaking, but was determined to crack that shell nonetheless.

Emma's stratagem worked far better than expected. Margarete discovered that she liked dancing with Eddie, and that dancing drove away her depression. Eddie was attracted to Margarete from the beginning and became increasingly enamored as she regained her confidence and vivacity. He also helped her brother, Hans, to reconnect with friends and worldly interests. Rosa at first was disturbed by Eddie's courtship, which she believed could only lead to further disappointment for Margarete, since he was not a Jew. But he gradually won her over with his charm, his helpfulness to Hans, and his veneration of Rosa Luxemburg. For more than a year Eddie's relationship with Margarete also seemed to be somewhat fraternal. But after they won first prize in a tango competition at the Alster Pavilion, it turned torrid.

Despite the government's disapproval of jazz and swing, Hans played swing tunes at the reception following the wedding of Margarete Singer and Erhard Ernst Emil Oestreicher. The wedding took place roughly a month after Chancellor Adolph Hitler rode in triumph through the streets of Hamburg and a year before the Nuremberg Laws of September 15, 1935, outlawed marriages between Jews and non-Jews.

Margarete and Eddie welcomed the birth of a daughter at Hamburg's famous Jewish Hospital two months after the Nuremberg decree, when the world's response to Germany's proudly announced persecution of its Jews could not be heard above the sound of falling leaves. Fortunately for me, the doctors at the hospital founded by the uncle of poet, Heinrich Heine, to heal people regardless of race, religion or nationality, ignored the government's orders to refuse to help Jewish babies who were having difficulty catching the breath of life.

Mother and Father before the war.

My grandmother with my father in 1902.

Chapter 3

Poisoned Air

Although the war against Jews was already underway when I was born, it didn't stop my mother and father from presenting me with two younger sisters, and it didn't stop us from laughing and playing together during our first few years. At the same time my parents were hostile witnesses to the parade of large and small restrictions that were decreed or enacted in the wake of Germany's rapid transformation from a democratic republic into a one-party dictatorship with apocalyptic ambitions. Hamburg had been the last city to convert to the Nazi ideology, and many Hamburgers were still skeptical despite their submission to it. Thousands suspected of opposing the regime were beaten and sent to nearby Neuengame Concentration Camp or killed. After a while, only a few people, including my parents and uncles, continued actively but secretly to resist.

I learned early on that neighbors were encouraged to inform on neighbors and that even private criticism of Nazi policy could be fatal if the authorities found out. A boy on our block had been promised a new bicycle by the secret police if he reported on his parent's private conversations and activities. After he complied, his parents were arrested and deported to a concentration camp, and the boy was left with no one to provide for him and no new bicycle. Shunned because of what he had done, the boy, too, eventually disappeared. The impression he left was indelible, though not as painful as one created about the same time by Monica, the girl who lived two floors below us, when she told me she would no longer play with me because I was a "Jew pig."

Because he was married to my mother, my father was a living affront to Nazi racial policy and the growing consensus that Jews were not fit to live with Aryans. For this apostasy he was subjected to increasing pressure to divorce Mother and abandon their children. Also, because he had been a confirmed internationalist until the Hitler-Stalin nonaggression pact in 1939 destroyed his faith in Communism, Father was doubly suspect in the eyes of Nazi Party and police officials and was the object of intense hostility by the brown-shirted thugs known as Storm Troopers.

Throughout the prewar years, Father wore his bad reputation with calm assurance, maintaining his marriage and his friendships with Jews as well as Gentiles, giving no one reason to think he was dispirited or even discouraged by official or communal hatreds. Unlike the arrogance of those in power, Father's obvious confidence was balanced by a genuine interest in others. Strangers as well as friends turned to him instinctively; beggars opened up to him, and he to them. He loved classical music, art, friendships, women, and jokes. His wit was seasoned by years of travel, reading, and a fascination with eccentric behavior and temperamental machinery. Eventually the Storm Troopers got to him. They tied him to a lamppost and beat him until they permanently injured his kidneys, and they told him that he and his Jewish family would be killed unless he divorced Mother and joined them. He placated them by agreeing to join the Luftwaffe.

Because the beating did not break Father's spirit, it did not make Mother or me more fearful for very long. She quickly recovered her outward air of defiance, and he very soon seemed to find a comfortable niche in the special procurement arm of the Luftwaffe, which made our entire family feel more secure. The deportations in November 1941, however, were devastating. Although I was only six at that time, I understood that the worst thing in the world that could happen to me would be to lose my mother, and that Mother's loss of her mother, her brother, and her aunt was unbearably painful. As further deportations of Jews occurred over the next year and a half, and the hate campaign against us intensified, I also understood that any day Mother might be taken as well. I watched and tried to help as she and Father did their best to find a way for us to live with all the hurt and anger and uncertainty. She remained defiantly proud in public but brooded much more frequently indoors. I managed to suppress my fear for her safety when we were together, but it inevitably emerged whenever we were separated.

With Mother's family gone, the authorities seemed to be closing in on Father's as well. His father had died at sea when he and his six brothers and two sisters were still quite young, forcing his mother to fend for the entire family. When grown each of the sons actively opposed the Nazi regime in one fashion or another. Earlier that summer Father's favorite brother, Eugene Oestreicher, had been arrested for aiding the Resistance while serving in the army in occupied France. Turned over to an SS unit known as the Ascension Commandos because of their reputation for killing those in their custody, Eugene had taken his own life rather than risk incriminating others. Shortly after his suicide, the Gestapo had searched a garret room Father rented in a Brussels pension and used for subversive activities. But while the police were making their way up the stairs, the chambermaid had saved his skin by quickly removing a batch of incriminating papers.

Father had laughed during his last visit as he told us about the heroic chambermaid and presented me with the licorice mask of Winston Churchill. Such stories not only thrilled me, they made it possible to imagine that the Nazis might not be as all-powerful as they appeared. But Mother understandably felt constrained to protest. "You can't keep taking such risks," she would say, reminding him that his brother, Eugene, had been arrested and had died in SS custody and that we would face deportation if Father was arrested.

Before returning to Belgium, however, Father succeeded in imparting his quiet but intense will to resist and his confidence that we would live to witness the downfall of the Nazis. Mother was then ready to face the Gestapo when she reported to them each week. Sometimes I had to go with her but only once had I seen her break down and weep. That had been shortly before the previous Christmas, when I had looked down an air shaft in the Gestapo offices and seen the bloodied face of Uncle Fred in the room below.

Uncle Fred was not my real uncle but my parents' friend, a huge, red-bearded bachelor who treated me as a favorite niece and always brought gifts—food and flowers for Mother, licorice and a flower for me. He lived with his mother, who was a member of an old Hamburg family, but his father, who was dead, had been from Scotland. The father ran the Hamburg office of a company that insured ship cargoes and had offices in Glasgow and Hamburg. As a boy, Uncle Fred had spent his summers and attended university in Scotland. Before his father died, Fred had served as an officer on a German freighter on which my father also sailed, and the two men had become good friends. After his father's death, Uncle Fred was extremely wealthy, with a Rolls Royce, a chauffeur, and a valet who trimmed and brushed his beautiful beard. He had his clothes made on Saville Row in London but was not fond of the English and accused them of having abused the Scots for centuries. Although German, he liked to wear the kilt, shawl, silver buckles, feathered cap and other strange attire of his father's family on occasions such as my parents' wedding.

I moved away from the air shaft without saying anything, but the smaller of the two Gestapo officials questioning Mother, a man whose hair was so pale it looked almost white, had seen me look and made Mother look too. He insisted that our friend was a British agent, and accused Mother of helping him.

Mother began to shake and cry out that they had made a terrible mistake, that Uncle Fred was as loyal as Hans Albers, Hamburg's favorite movie actor. She said they must be mad to think he was a spy.

The official calmly stepped forward and slapped her face like a woman who has been insulted by a man's crude remark. Then he shouted, "We ask the questions! We decide who is loyal and who is mad!"

Mother quickly agreed and apologized, but insisted that their informer must have been mistaken.

The larger official interrupted her and then both men questioned her about our relationship with Uncle Fred. Mother told them he was named after King Frederick of Prussia and that Father always called him "Barbarossa" because of his name and red hair. She said Father knew him because he was connected with a shipping company Father had worked for years ago. She tried to add that she believed he was a patriotic German, but she was cut short.

"He admitted that he talks to the British as well as Jews," the smaller agent said, "which means he is a traitor twice over!"

"He has family and property in Scotland," Mother pointed out.

"We told you that he has already confessed!" the larger man shouted, pounding his fist into his hand. He threatened that we would be executed with Uncle Fred unless Mother also confessed everything she knew about him. He said this with bone-chilling matter-of-factness. When Mother insisted that she knew nothing, he suddenly grabbed a handful of my hair, pulled my head sharply down to one side and shouted at me to tell what "the traitor" and my parents talked about.

I protested that Uncle Fred was not a traitor and would never hurt the Fatherland.

The agent shook my head and said I didn't have a Fatherland. Then he let go of my hair and said Mother and I would be allowed to go home as soon as I told him what he wanted to know. He added that I would get a nice little present besides.

His last remark reminded me of the boy down the street from us who had been promised a new bicycle in return for information about his parents. I said that my father was in the Luftwaffe and wouldn't talk to a spy.

The Gestapo agent replied that any man who would marry a Jew would talk to Germany's enemies.

"My mother is pretty," was all I could think to say. Furious tears began to run down my cheeks as the agent laughed.

I hated him for laughing even more than for twisting my hair. But the two men eventually tired of us and let us go home. Before we left, however, they told me to return with Mother the following week.

* * *

All week long we worried about Frederick and dreaded another interrogation. But when we returned there were more than a dozen other Jewish children and mothers standing outside the building, looking cold and frightened. Several helmeted soldiers also were there, two of them holding large German shepherds. No one seemed to know why we had been rounded up, but all feared that we would be deported. One mother thought that we might be put to work clearing snow or placing sandbags around official buildings, the sorts of tasks performed by some of the thousands of war prisoners forced to labor in Hamburg's factories and streets. Another mother silenced speculation by suggesting that, since it was the Christmas season, we might be compelled to sing "Silent Night" for soldiers or possibly prisoners. But minutes later, an SS officer told us that because Jewish children had been excluded from public school training on the use of gas masks, we would receive such instruction now, during the Christmas recess, while the facilities were not in use. Children of mixed

My parents, Margarete and Edward Oestreicher.

marriages were being taken first, he said, which prompted one of the women in the group to comment that Hamburg's program to prepare children for a poison gas attack was well known and quite safe.

But when we emerged from a truck after bouncing about for half an hour, we were surprised to see even more soldiers and dogs surrounding a clearing in front of fairly dense woods. About twenty yards in front of a line of scrawny pines there was a small hut or shed. On a small rise to the left was a machine gun surrounded by sandbags. Beyond that the long barrel of an anti-aircraft cannon pointed at the leaden sky. The soldiers nearest the machine gun were standing and smoking or drinking something hot, paying little attention to us. One mother exclaimed that she didn't think this was the same place the authorities used to train the Gentile children. None of the others disagreed.

The Commanding Officer told us the gas masks being issued by the soldiers were the same ones used by Aryan children and that it didn't matter if they didn't fit well. Mine was much too large for me. While he was talking to the group, Mother quickly braided my hair, tightened the straps of the mask, and tucked the braids under the sides. When it still wasn't snug enough she took off her leather gloves and stuffed them over the braids inside the mask. The soldiers made us line up before the door to the building with the tallest in front and the rest behind according to height. I was near the end, in front of a small boy in an oversized mask. The soldiers then herded the mothers to a spot about twenty yards away and told them to be silent so that we could hear the instructions. The Commander shouted for us to pay attention to him and held aloft a silver whistle, which was difficult to see through the lenses of the masks which were fogging up on the inside.

The Commander told us that we were to go inside the building and wait quietly until we heard him blow his whistle. He demonstrated the whistle with a shrill blast that made us shiver.

After we heard the whistle, he explained, we should remove our masks and then we would be allowed to come outside. But no one would be allowed to leave until all masks had been removed.

As he repeated the instructions, adding that if we didn't do it right we would have to repeat the exercise, I looked about and noticed that the machine gunners were attending their weapons and the other soldiers, except for two near the door, had formed a line in front of our mothers.

"Attention!" the Commander shouted, and the door to the shed was opened.

We filed somewhat hesitantly into a room with very little light and hoped the Commander would whistle soon so we could get out of there. He waited for what seemed like forever, and some of the children began to stumble about, moan beneath their masks or fall to the floor. Finally he let loose a long blast and some of the children removed their masks. Several screamed and thrashed about while the rest of us pushed toward the door and began to pound on it wildly. I was near the door but was knocked off my feet. Holding on to my mask, I looked desperately for a shaft of light. In addition to the pandemonium inside I heard pounding and screaming on the other side of the door accompanied by barking and machine gun fire. When the door crashed inward I crawled toward the daylight over the other children. Before I could see clearly, Mother grabbed me up and we plunged into the woods, managing in the noise and great confusion to escape. When we paused to catch our breaths, we could still hear sounds of screaming and occasional gunfire, and I saw that one of Mother's hands was bleeding, making ribbon patterns in the snow.

She said she must have cut it on the door but that I shouldn't worry. She asked about me and, after I assured her that I was not injured and could breathe normally, said she thought she knew where we were and what direction to take to get home. We looked back anxiously at the trail of blood and footprints we had left behind. Mother stuffed her bleeding hand into a glove, and we started walking, trying at first to step under the cover of dense pines where there was little snow, so as not to leave such an obvious trail. A couple of hours later we reached a street that ran into Hasselbrook Strasse only a few blocks from our apartment. After resting in the apartment for a brief time, Mother retrieved Rena from Cousin Inge. I suppose Mother told Inge what we had been through, but we never talked about it again and never read or heard any explanations of what had happened. I felt sure that many of the mothers and children must have been wounded or killed, and wondered what had happened to the other survivors, if there were any.

When it was time again for her to report to the Gestapo, Mother talked about not going since it was possible the police thought we had been killed during this incident. But she went anyway because she knew the authorities were meticulous about accounting for everything and everyone, including corpses. Besides, unless we had a foolproof place to hide, citizens, like the two women who had recently denounced a Jewish woman living in the Winterhude district, would most likely report us. The denounced woman was married to a non-Jew. She had offended her neighbors by slipping some food to a hungry Russian prisoner of war who was engaged in forced labor on her street. Mother didn't tell me what transpired on her succeeding visits to the Gestapo, but I became increasingly apprehensive about her safety whenever we were separated. This fear surfaced while I was taking Rena to Cousin Inge's apartment, impelling me to disobey Mother's instructions and return home.

* * *

If Mother didn't wake by morning I resolved to take Rena to Cousin Inge's apartment without further delay. Mother was still warm, even moist to the touch, and I felt increasingly optimistic that she would awaken at some point. But I knew that I needed help. I couldn't telephone—our line had been disconnected by the authorities much earlier. I felt certain, however, that Inge would be able to contact my father. Tall, attractive and resourceful, she was the daughter of his half-brother and had been our communications link in the past. She also had looked after Rena on occasion and had been the one to take Helga to live with an Aryan family. Her parents had a grocery store beneath their apartment, and though there were small swastika flags in the store window, they also had a Jewish woman living in their apartment.

Chapter 4

Awakening

I was awakened in the morning by the sound of moaning and looked over to see Mother pulling at the neckline of her dress. Her eyes were still closed but Rena's were open and she was quietly talking to a rag doll I had placed near her. I lifted her gently with the doll and placed her on Mother's chest. Moments later Mother opened her eyes and tried to remove my startled sister before realizing what she had in her hands. When she became fully conscious, she kissed and hugged Rena and held her against her breast.

Mother didn't explain why she had tried to take her life, and I didn't ask while she was still weak, on the verge of tears and having difficulty standing or moving about. But I am sure I would have asked if an unexpected visitor hadn't arrived within an hour of her awakening. Since no one had called on us in weeks, the sudden knocking startled and frightened us, until we heard my cousin Inge's voice on the other side of the door.

"I was so worried about you," Inge said, still breathing hard after climbing up the stairs. She explained that the Jewish woman living in her apartment had received a deportation order yesterday and had taken her own life. Inge said she feared that we had received such an order and would have come sooner but couldn't get away.

I looked at Mother and I understood in that instant, even before she explained, that we also had received a deportation order. In a few days we were supposed to report to Moorweide Park, the place from which our Jewish relatives had been taken along with almost all the other Jews in Hamburg. Mother told Inge that, in a desperate bid to save her children, she had asked me to take Rena to Inge's home and then had tried to take her own life, hoping the authorities would not go further after finding her dead. Inge didn't say anything but simply leaned forward and took Mother's hand. The two women sat down and searched each other's eyes and then began to talk while I made tea from the packet of food Inge had brought. They continued to talk even after the air-raid alarms started blaring shortly after our grandfather clock, which had been made by my great grandfather, struck noon. Unlike us, Cousin Inge could have gone to a shelter because she was a Gentile. But she didn't move, even when the second, more compelling series of alarms warned that Allied bombers were expected to arrive within fifteen minutes.

"It must be the Americans," Inge observed, quietly underscoring the fact that the American bombers usually came during the day and the British by night.

I kept expecting her to go to a shelter. There was a massive concrete bunker several stories high within easy walking distance and a smaller brick shelter even closer. She could also have been admitted to the shelter in the basement of our building. Neither Mother nor I would have thought less of her for doing what we could not. But Inge continued to sit with us as the minutes ticked away. I served the tea but couldn't help remarking that it was ten minutes since the second alarm had sounded. Cousin Inge thanked me for the tea, which she stirred pensively and began to sip as if it were too precious to be put aside for an air raid. When the all-clear sounded a few minutes later, however, Cousin Inge drained her cup in one swallow and stood up.

"Thank heaven that's over," she said. "It's time I got back home." She smiled and so did we. Her eyes were a glistening turquoise as she told us goodbye, promising that she would let Father know about the deportation order as soon as possible. When she left, Inge took Rena with her, along with a bag filled with Rena's clothes and dolls.

* * *

That night it was unnaturally hot even for the last week of July, and breathlessly still despite the distant flashing of dry lightning. Mother and I went to bed soon after sunset. Although I was tired and glad to be in the same bed with her, I couldn't sleep because of the heat and because Mother soon began writhing and gasping and occasionally crying out in her sleep. I didn't know whether this was because of all the gas she had inhaled or because she was so upset by our deportation order. Both thoughts distressed me and I was still wide awake less than an hour later when the air-raid sirens began to wail again. This time I counted while the sirens sang out three alarms of fifteen seconds each, with five-second intervals in between. This signaled that Allied bombers were expected within half an hour.

Although we couldn't use the shelters, I knew that Hamburgers were proud of the elaborate air defenses that had seen them through more than a hundred and thirty air raids. As engineers, machinists, shipyard, factory, and foundry workers they made a lot of the defensive hardware, including the radar devices that tracked enemy bombers practically from the time they left the coast of England. And they were almost as admiring of the interceptor aircraft as they were of the men who flew them. Photos of fighter pilots, the new Teutonic knights, were in every newspaper and magazine, and it was a point of civic pride that Germany's most coveted reward for extraordinary heroism was a few nights in Hamburg's renowned red light district.

Mother's energetic response to the air-raid sirens indicated that, despite the deportation order, she had fully recovered her will to live. She leapt out of bed after the first wail, turned on our radio and began to run water in the tub so that we would have a supply in case it was shut off after the bombs started falling. She also checked the hallway to make sure a bucket of sand and a fire extinguisher were available and then began to boil two of the three eggs Inge had brought. But we were both relieved when the all-clear sounded minutes later. Much as we wanted the Allies to defeat Germany, we were terrified when bombs fell in our neighborhood and horrified when a nearby children's hospital was hit. At such times I was in a state of emotional turmoil, simultaneously hating both the bombing of residential neighborhoods and the murderous conduct of the Nazi regime that was being attacked. Thankful that there had been little or no damage this night, I gave my licorice mask of Winston Churchill a long lick and we went back to bed. The night was so quiet I could hear a family returning from our air-raid shelter, rolling their children and supplies in a small wagon with iron wheels.

A few hours later we were awakened by another series of alarms. Barely five minutes later there was a second warning—a short blast of the sirens repeated fifteen times a minute—followed by a radio announcement for Hamburgers to go immediately to their shelters. The announcer was known fondly as Uncle Valerian because of his soothing tones and confident manner. But there was alarming urgency in his voice as he warned that a large fleet of Allied bombers was arriving within a few minutes. Each time he repeated the order he was more emphatic. I glanced at Mother, who was staring at Rena's empty bed. I tried to reassure her by pointing out that Cousin Inge would surely take Rena to an air-raid shelter.

Mother unpacked two woolen blankets from a trunk at the foot of the bed and took them into the bathroom to soak in the tub in case we needed to protect ourselves from fire. I put on a smocked dress, heavier and more protective than the one I had taken off earlier. There was no Mogen David on it, but I knew from past experience that this wouldn't stop some people from identifying us as Jews, apparently because both Mother and I had very dark hair and eyes.

Looking out a window toward the Eilbeck canal the first thing I noticed was that the sky was almost clear except for a few high clouds and a large moon which I couldn't see but which I assumed was full because the clock on a distant steeple was clearly visible. As soon as the frantic alarms went quiet, the *ack-ack* battery on the Alster cracked out two quick test rounds to let everybody know they were at their battle station. Echoing barks from other batteries indicated they too were ready for combat. Beams of light probed the lowest clouds, searching for the Mosquito bombers buzzing overhead. Then, suddenly, the crews began to shift and jerk the beams about as if they were out of control. Simultaneously the *ack-ack* batteries launched an ear-shattering barrage that didn't last very long but filled the sky with tiny puffs of smoke. The moon seemed to have fallen to earth, bathing everything in light so intense that I could read the time on a steeple clock. It was just past twelve thirty. I ran to a window that faced in the direction of the Alster, since the dazzling light seemed to be coming from that direction, and saw that it wasn't the moon but hundreds of flares in Christmas-tree clusters, smoking a bit as they slowly descended.

Overhead the first wave of British heavy bombers droned like a chorus of celestial pipe organs. This dirge was soon interrupted by a series of explosions, apparently in the St. Pauli district, where revelries famously continued during air raids despite Uncle Valerian's stern counseling. All too soon bombs began to fall near enough that I could also hear their high-pitched whistles. Not content with the unnerving whine bombs normally made as they fell, the British had added a device which produced a blood-curdling sound that built in intensity as the bomb descended. Although I hadn't heard her call out, I knew Mother didn't want me to stand in the window during the raid. But it was difficult to take my eyes from the sight of the universe exploding. Returning to bed I held on to Mother as the

An Allied bomber in an exploding sky over Hamburg. (Source: Imperial War Museum)

bombing continued for more than two hours. Finally the all-clear sirens began to wail and the thunder of explosions was succeeded by the anguished braying of fire engines, ambulances and other emergency vehicles.

Remembering a thud directly above our heads during the raid, Mother and I went up a short flight of stairs to the attic, a storage space for tenants, now empty as a fire precaution. Mother carried a flashlight and a hand-pump fire extinguisher. As soon as we entered we saw a jagged hole in the roof and something that looked like a piece of bent pipe among wood splinters and shards of tile on the floor. There were no flames or smoke but Mother doused the pipe and surrounding area with the liquid in the extinguisher. Then we got a bucket of sand and covered the pipe as best we could. Because the roof was sloped Mother was able to put her head through the hole to look around for signs of fire on the roof.

"Oh, my God!" she exclaimed. After a minute or so she lifted me up so I could see. Across the city thousands of fires were burning, most of them a considerable distance from us, but some only a few blocks away. Although it was not yet dawn, coils of smoke were clearly visible and not just the smell, but even the taste of soot entered our open mouths. We went back to our apartment but there was no possibility of sleeping with the turmoil outside and within. I could see that Mother was worrying about Rena, since there had seemed to be a lot of fire in the direction of Inge's home. She lived near the part of Alster Lake that had been covered with netting to mislead the bombers into dropping their bombs in the water. Her street was named Brandsende, because many years earlier a terrible fire in the heart of the city had halted there. Although I reminded Mother that the street was lucky, we went out to see for ourselves.

Walking toward the Alster and Brandsende, we passed hundreds of people in the streets talking about the raid and inspecting their neighborhood for damage. Everybody was shouting because of the noise and the excitement over the magnitude of the raid and the destruction. We heard that Hamburg's air defenses, including the Luftwaffe, had been totally ineffective because the British had dropped metal foil that had somehow jammed all the radar. This seemed exceedingly farfetched. But several blocks later, I spotted a large strip of foil draped like Christmas tinsel over an evergreen branch. I picked it up and took it with me. On a block that had been hit by a high-explosive bomb, prisoners in striped clothing were helping to look for bodies under the smoldering rubble.

When we reached the Alster we could see huge fires raging on the far side. We also discovered that incendiary bombs had in fact set fire to the camouflage netting that had covered part of the lake. An elderly fire warden wearing an old-fashioned spiked helmet told us that the anti-aircraft battery on a barge in the lake had suffered a direct hit. The entire crew had been killed. He confirmed the rumor that the city's air defenses had been knocked out by some new radar-jamming device. When I showed him my piece of tin foil, he examined it carefully and refused to give it back. Probably recognizing us as Jews, he pointed to an area across the lake devoid of flames.

"You can see that the English spared the Jewish district," he said, fuming.

"But there are only Nazis living there now," Mother reminded him.

We continued walking to Brandsende and saw that it had once again been spared. We didn't try to make contact with Inge then because Mother was satisfied that Rena was better off with her and we didn't want nosy neighbors to realize that Rena belonged with us.

On the way home we passed hundreds of people sitting or lying on the ground outside St. George Hospital. Most were children with their mothers. Many were coughing and a few were bloodied. It reminded me that a hospital for children in a nearby district had been destroyed in a raid two years earlier. I had been in that hospital sick with pneumonia before it was bombed. A family friend, a woman whose father was a high city official, had arranged to have me admitted as her niece. For the three nights I was there Mother had dreamed that I was behind a brick wall in an area engulfed with flames and that she could hear me calling but couldn't get over the wall. So, even though I was still having difficulty breathing, she had slipped into that hospital wearing a shawl over her Star of David and had taken me home. A night or so later, incendiary bombs had set fire to the hospital and many of the children had been killed. Now looking at the children on the grass beside St. George I felt sorry for the injured and hoped they wouldn't have to be taken to a hospital far from home. At the same time I envied them for being able to get drinking water from an emergency supply being dispensed there. Mother and I didn't dare ask for some.

As we left the area we heard an ambulance driver tell a nurse that there were more than a thousand dead on the other side of the lake and that many more people were trapped and might not be saved because the water pressure was too low to put out the fires in the area. Returning to our apartment in the largely unscathed Eilbeck District, Mother told a woman in the courtyard of our building about the hole in the roof and the metal object on the attic floor. She asked the woman to inform a warden but the woman didn't respond, perhaps because we were the only ones still living on the top floor or perhaps because it was Sunday morning and she was on her way to church.

We hadn't been back in our apartment more than an hour or so when air-raid sirens suddenly began warning that more bombers were on the way. Like everyone else I hoped that it was a false alarm and wondered how the firefighters and rescue workers who were battling hundreds of fires would react. Mother and I watched from a window as the first waves of American Flying Fortresses passed overhead after dropping thousands of tons of bombs on harbor areas.

Mother said that the Americans were after the U-boats, trying to persuade me that we weren't targets even though we could see bombers almost directly above us.

Hamburg's history as a seaport circulated in the bloodstream of all its citizens. Storied pirates were our true patron saints. Here the world's largest and fastest passenger liners and battleships had been built, and from here many of the liners had sailed as part of the fleet of the world's largest shipping line. As in the city's cultural achievements, Jews figured prominently in the naval legend. A brilliant Jew named Ballin had steered the local shipping line into preeminence as the world's largest. My love of the harbor and the sea had little to do with Ballin, however, but was passed to me from my father, who had made the sea his university. I wanted to do the same when I grew up. Despite wartime secrecy, like everybody else I was aware that since the scuttling of the battleship Bismarck in Montevideo Bay, Hamburg's shipworkers had been building mainly submarines. Unlike others, I wasn't proud that Winston Churchill had said these U-boats, which hunted in packs like wolves, were a greater danger than the Blitz. But I dearly hoped the American bombers had been listening to him and were dropping all their bombs on the submarine pens. I said as much to my licorice mask but didn't think it could hear me over the thundering explosions that were moving steadily nearer like a natural storm.

It was early afternoon when the all-clear finally sounded and our Aryan neighbors emerged blinking, coughing, and cursing from their bunkers. A huge pillar of black smoke was blowing inland from the harbor obscuring the sun and stinging our eyes. A swelling chorus of rescue vehicles seemed to be trying to reassure those in need that help was on the way. Above their din I could hear the low moan of ship foghorns. I wondered if the ships were calling for help or fleeing the city and wished that we could be on one heading for the open sea. I could see from Mother's expression that she was worried

A sunken ship, one of 2,900 destroyed, impedes traffic in Hamburg harbor after the bombing. (Source: U.S. National Archives and Records Administration)

about Rena but the chaos in the streets must have convinced her that we wouldn't get far if we tried to go to Brandsende.

Mosquito Bombers made sure that no one slept in Hamburg that night. Exhausted firefighters, slave laborers, soldiers, and volunteers were still battling conflagrations and pulling people out of hot rubble shortly before midnight when the alarms started wailing for the third time that day. Soon, repetitive blasts herded bleating Gentiles back into the shelters where they had spent most of their bloody Sabbath. Mother and I laid on the bed and read by flashlight until the all-clear sounded. Soon after we removed the blackout drapes and heard our neighbors sheepishly returning to their apartments.

The desire to be on a boat leaving Hamburg took over my imagination again. I listened for the deep, strong voices of ships telling other boats that they were moving on despite the darkness. We needed to find a boat that would take us some place safe from the Gestapo. Maybe Father could arrange it, I thought, if he reached us in time.

In the morning, smoke still rose in thick columns in several areas, but the flames that had been so dramatic in the night appeared to have diminished substantially. Emergency crews were still working furiously to save people and portions of the city when Mother and I set out to check on conditions at Brandsende and to find out if Inge had been able to get in touch with Father. Although it was against the law, Mother wore a light shawl to hide her Mogen David. We didn't get very far before we began to encounter buildings that had been hit by bombs. To our great relief, Brandsende appeared to be untouched. But Inge's block was so filled with police and soldiers that we didn't attempt to enter. Instead, we turned and walked down Rosenstrasse, the street on which Mother had lived as a child, and then turned again into Paul Strasse, where Aunt Emma had lived before she was deported. Glad that neither of these short streets had been severely damaged, we started home.

We didn't get far, however, before we were forced to detour through Hammerbrook, a residential area closer to the Elbe River. Although shipyards and housing developments a bit farther downstream had been devastated, the only visible sign of suffering here was the smoke that hung about these streets keeping most of the residents indoors. When air-raid sirens started wailing again, most people must have thought it was still too early in the morning to be anything but another false alarm. Except for us no one began to run for shelter. But only ten minutes later American Flying Fortresses arrived in force and this time they seemed to be starting with the Hammerbrook harbor area. In the general pandemonium that developed we tried to wedge our way inside a medieval looking brick tower that served as an air-raid shelter. But a warden stopped us. He didn't object that we were Jewish but that we didn't have passes to use that shelter. Perhaps ironically, he pointed us toward a church steeple in the distance and told us to take shelter there. As scores of explosions in rapid succession devastated the streets we had just walked through, we reached the fortress-like walls of the church and found an open door.

The ceiling inside was high and arched and supported by huge stone pillars in rows a few yards from walls with large stained-glass windows. In gloom slashed by beams of light, a clump of about a dozen people knelt before a large gleaming cross with the tortured figure of the crucified Christ looking down on them. A rack holding rows of flickering candles stood off to one side. On the wall above the rack was a plaster figure of a woman holding a baby. She had yellow hair topped by a gold crown and the baby had a gold disk behind his head. Although this was the first time I had been in such a grand church, I didn't have to be told that the woman was Mary, holding her baby, Jesus. I had seen pictures of them many times before in our illustrated bible at home, but I was slightly puzzled by the crown and yellow hair, until I remembered that my middle sister, Helga, had even lighter hair.

The bombs were still fairly close but the noise was not as great inside the thick walls, and I felt more solidly protected than during any other air raid. In contrast to the flames outside, the flickering candles were reassuring, almost mesmerizing, in their calm assertion that no amount of destruction could diminish the beauty of their tiny gifts of light. But while I was marveling at the magnificence of our sanctuary, inhaling the musty odors of stone and burnt incense, some among those praying were looking our way and whispering to one another. Very soon one of the women got up and began to whisper in the ear of a rather large man dressed in black kneeling in front of them. Slowly, perhaps reluctantly, the man rose up and came over to confront us.

He told us that we would have to leave immediately, since it was forbidden to give shelter to Jews.

I looked and saw that Mother had lost her scarf, so that the Mogen David with the inscription "JUDE" was visible even in the dim light.

Mother pleaded with the man to let us stay longer, promising to leave as soon as the bombing stopped. She told him that no one would know we had been there.

In reply, the man nodded toward the people who had stopped praying to stare at us. Two or three rose and approached us, looking first surprised and then reproachful.

"What about her?" I asked, aiming a finger at the figure of the Virgin Mary. I wanted the others to see me, and for once Mother didn't grab my finger to stop me from pointing.

The priest looked puzzled.

"Isn't she a Jew?" I demanded, speaking loud enough for the others to hear.

The prelate sputtered, trying at first to answer my question but quickly giving up and insisting that we leave immediately.

I continued to point at the statue as he raised his arms and herded us back down the long hall to the main door of the church. Outside, the bombing seemed to have stopped and we started walking toward home, feeling that we had managed to use the church after all to get through the raid. But then the alarm sounded again and we started running, madly trying to get as close to home as we could before the next wing of Flying Fortresses arrived overhead. In front of us a flight of fighter planes snarled and hissed like enraged cats clawing the air to get at the Americans.

A few Mosquito Bombers tormented Hamburgers again that night, sending them repeatedly to shelters that must have smelled of the sweat of fear. Mother was terribly unhappy that we had not seen Rena or found out whether Inge had been able to reach Father. We didn't talk about the deportation order but knew it was a ticking bomb that would soon explode. Lying in bed later that night I thought about our experience in the church. The medieval atmosphere, unreal smell and evocation of people and events from very long ago had stirred my imagination. Remembering that Father's Bible was on our bookshelf, I quickly fetched it and held up a colored illustration close to our shawl-covered lamp. It showed Mary, a young Jewish mother wearing a plain shawl and clutching a baby to her chest, hurrying away from the walled gate of a city. Behind her, Joseph, a rather gnarled carpenter, was looking back fearfully at soldiers brandishing bloody weapons on the ramparts of the wall. One of the soldiers held up the severed head of a child. A lock of raven hair streamed from under Mary's shawl and her large, dark eyes looked fiercely protective as she strode toward the light. Although the infant had a halo, the picture affirmed my feeling that the gold crown, blond hair and languid expression of the Mary in the church were not authentic.

Having been kept awake until almost two o'clock by the Mosquitoes, Mother and I slept late on Tuesday morning. When we were ready to go to Inge's, the air-raid sirens began to wail once more. Although the Americans didn't show up, the warnings were repeated throughout the day. Around noon, there was a loud knocking on our door and I raced to open it, thinking Father or Inge had arrived. Instead it was a policeman accompanied by Herr Wiederman, the Nazi block captain and housemaster for our apartment building, as well as the father of my former friend, Monika. They were checking to make sure that we would report as scheduled to the park on Moorweide Strasse, the place all Hamburg had come to know as the staging area for the final expulsion of Jews. The policeman said that Mother should bring her three children with her, which touched off a fierce argument between them.

Mother lied to the policeman, telling him that my middle sister, Helga, was not her daughter and hence not a Jew. She said that Helga had been reclaimed by her Aryan mother and was living far from Hamburg. When the policeman demanded to know where Helga was hidden, Mother insisted that the authorities knew where they lived but that she didn't. Mother said she thought the real mother was Bavarian and persuaded Herr Wiederman to support her story, pointing out that he would have been remiss in not reporting Helga's departure if she were a Jew.

"She's clearly an Aryan," Wiederman said of Helga, emphasizing her blond hair and blue eyes and even comparing her to his own daughter.

The policeman was not happy with the situation and was even angrier when Mother told him that Rena was with her Aryan grandmother in Friesland on the North Sea. The policeman insisted that Mother must bring Rena with us to the Moorweide. Mother demanded that he tell her how she could accomplish that, pointing out that we weren't allowed to travel, not even by bicycle.

The policeman continued to bully Mother until the wailing of air-raid sirens stopped him short. Before hurrying off, he demanded Grandmother's address. Mother made up something and after the all-clear she told me she had changed her mind about going to see Inge. She said that the risk was too great that Rena would be linked to us.

I could see from her grim expression that she was very distressed about what would happen when the time came to report to the Moorweide. Although the bombing had been worse than any that had been experienced before, it hadn't dampened the Nazis determination to get rid of Jews. I tried in vain to think of something encouraging to say after she closed the door, but the prospect of deportation made our apartment feel like a jail cell for the condemned.

A view of a shattered Hamburg neighborhood. (Credit: Oxfordian Kissuth)

Chapter 5

Gomorrah

Tuesday night was hot, without a breeze to flush out the smoke that had continued to rise from the fires caused by Sunday's and Monday's raids. I was still awake when the sirens started again half an hour before midnight. Although the alarm was supposed to let us know bombers were thirty minutes away, almost immediately Christmas-tree flares made it clear that time had run out. Mother and I quickly dressed as the first detonations thundered in the near distance. We filled a couple of pots with drinking water. Then Mother soaked two wool blankets in the bathtub water and I stuffed my ears with cotton wads. As anti-aircraft cannons boomed at planes that seemed to be directly overhead, we got back into bed and despite the heat put pillows over our faces to protect them and help to muffle the horrendous noise.

An explosion shook the building seconds later. Walls, ceiling and windows shattered and showered us with plaster and glass. Lamps and picture frames were hurled around the room. A second blast sent gale-force winds gusting through the apartment, crashing the front door onto the floor, stripping molding, sills and sashes, overturning bookcases and tables. Then a sheet of flame flashed

British heavy bombers on their way to or from Hamburg.

outside our window as a third explosion seemed to detonate inside my skull. The shock wave sent our bed skittering across the room until it tipped and spilled us onto the floor.

I was stunned. I couldn't catch my breath and desperately had to empty my bladder, but I was too worried about Mother to stay on the floor for long. The air was thick with plaster dust and the floor slippery with broken glass. As I urinated on a crumpled heap of rug, managing somehow to remain upright and keep my panties dry, I thought I could see Mother doing the same in another corner. I tried to call out to her but we were entirely surrounded by screaming bombs and explosions. Through a large hole that had been a window I watched as the balconies of the building next door were sprayed with shards of white phosphorous, some landing on table tops where they glowed and smoldered like strange food from outer space. Every geranium on every balcony was clearly visible in the glare of the flames. As I searched for my shoes, an incendiary bomb thudded through the roof of our building. I found one shoe and Mother the other. Unable to speak, we embraced and felt one another all over. Finding that nothing seemed to be broken or missing, we retrieved our dampened blankets and cautiously picked our way down the darkened, debris-cluttered stairway toward the courtyard at the bottom.

Draping the blankets over our heads like huge shawls, we ran to the large metal door that led to the basement shelter. Mother took the nozzle of a fire extinguisher and banged on the door until it opened. A man's head in a large steel helmet poked out. It was our block warden, Herr Wiederman. "What are you doing here?" he demanded.

An earsplitting explosion answered and he slammed the door. Mother banged some more and Herr Wiederman's head reappeared. We wedged our way inside.

"You have to let us stay!" Mother shouted, "We've been bombed out! It's certain death outside!"

The door to our apartment building's air-raid shelter, for Aryans only.

Several of the people lying or sitting on bunks in the shelter got up and came over to the door. One, a rumpled, whiskered walrus of a man, held a lantern near Mother's face.

"It's the Jews!" a woman shouted. "The Jews! The damned Jews!"

The voice was neither young nor old and there was no quality of mercy in it. In fact it seemed that the woman had progressed from surprise to indignation to outrage as she repeated herself. Explosions smothered whatever else she said and I desperately hoped others would be more compassionate; the explosions, although horrific, were much less frightening inside the bunker. But the next voice to rise above the din was Frau Wiederman's. She yelled at her husband, telling him he had to put us out because he was in charge and it was his duty to enforce the rules against sheltering Jews.

"You'll be held responsible!" she yelled. "Think of us! Think of your family!"

"Think of us, Daddy!" It was Monika, my former playmate. She was holding her favorite doll tightly and turning slightly away as if she feared I might try to snatch it from her. And she was wrinkling her nose. "Think of us!"

The man with the lantern spoke up, his voice and breath thick with schnapps. "Listen to your family! Put the Jews out!"

"They're going to be deported in two days," Herr Wiederman said, "I've seen the order myself."

"All the more reason to boot them out," the walrus man said.

Herr Wiederman turned to tell us to leave, but Mother interrupted, pleading with him and with the others to allow me, at least, to stay, an idea that was very upsetting to me but seemed to find some support within. To my relief, louder voices shouted down the soft-hearted.

"The Bolshevik Jews are behind this!" a hoarse voice growled. "They sold us out. They told the English where to bomb."

I found the idea exciting, but Mother said it was ridiculous.

"My husband is in the Luftwaffe," Mother shouted. "He's on his way here now. You will have to answer to him if you put us out!"

The response was angry insistence on our immediate expulsion. Frau Wiederman gave her husband a shove and he pushed open the door. Instead of going out, Mother stepped deeper inside the shelter.

"You will answer!" she shouted, and the room became silent. She didn't say anything more, but stood for several seconds looking into their faces, her dark eyes glistening in the lantern light. She looked hurt and angry, but cleansed of fear, almost triumphant. Many of the faces in the gloom began to look fearfully at us, apparently sensing that they had damned themselves by refusing to share their private dungeon. When another explosion rocked the building, Mother bent down with a calm, protective look and adjusted my blanket so that it covered my head. Herr Wiederman grabbed her arm to force her toward the door, but she wrenched free. Then she picked me up and walked into the street as the door slammed behind us.

A false dawn lit the southeastern sky, rouging Mother's cheeks and painting the walls of the buildings on our side of the street a glowing, lurid red. Through the openings of blasted windows we could see orange and yellow flames dancing beside pianos, making bonfires of bookcases, curling around bedposts. A torrent of hot wind coursed down Hasselbrook Strasse, bending trees almost double, stripping off branches and leaves and tugging at our blankets. Although anti-aircraft guns banged away and searchlights still probed the sky, the bombing seemed to have diminished. Along the street a geyser of water rose more than three feet above the pavement. Everything was unreal. We went back through the arched entrance to our courtyard and saw pink tulips of flame sprouting along the roofline not far from our apartment.

There were firemen in the street, which was encouraging because they normally didn't come out of their shelters while a raid was in progress. The firemen had unraveled a hose but it was flat. Although some water pressure had been restored after the raids Sunday and

The rear entrance to the courtyard of our building after the firestorm.

A rear view of our apartment building after the firestorm.

An opened door to our apartment building.

Monday, bunker-busting bombs had ruptured the mains during the first waves of this raid, creating geysers like the one we had just seen.

Some firemen across the street were working with crowbars to open the metal door of a cellar shelter, while a fireman at the top of a long ladder chopped a hole in the roof of the building next door. Although we were afraid to approach for fear of being reported, I went close enough to hear one fireman yell to another that smoke from the building had entered the shelter through an exit tunnel. I thought how horrible it must be for those suffocating inside the shelter and was glad for a moment to be outside. But even as the firemen succeeded in opening the shelter door and began bringing people outside, the terrifying shrieks of falling bombs, followed by thundering explosions, announced a new wave of Lancasters or Halifaxes. Both my eardrums seemed to burst at once as a large bomb landed much too close. The blast also collapsed the wall of the building next to the shelter. We watched and moaned "NO! NO! NO!" as the fireman who had chopped a hole in the roof fell with his ladder into the flames.

More bombs struck in quick succession. Most of the firemen abandoned the shelter victims and began to run for their own shelter. Two who didn't run were ripped apart by shrapnel or flying debris from another explosion. One fell on his face on top of a smoke victim and the other sat down on the sidewalk, holding his groin and screaming. Two firemen returned to retrieve their comrade and carry him in the direction of their bunker. Many of the shelter victims were lying where they had been placed on the grassy strip beside the street, but some were staggering about, coughing and blinded, clutching at trees or lampposts for support. We lay in the gutter and watched as two or three from the shelter chased after the firemen. Following another nearby explosion, we got up and hurried after them, hoping that the firemen might allow us into their bunker. We ran down a narrow side street between high walls of flame until we came to a large commercial avenue. The firemen's bunker was on

Father wrote, "Does anyone know the whereabouts of my family?" on our apartment building in Hamburg.

the other side, about fifty yards away, but the air blowing down the avenue was filled with flying embers and was so strong that I could hardly stand up. I lost my footing and would have gone tumbling into the flames, had Mother not held on to my hand and hauled me back to her side. We ducked back around the corner just as another bomb exploded between the firemen's bunker and us, spraying shrapnel into the wall we crouched behind.

After we'd caught our breath, we started running again, wanting desperately to get away from the flames and explosions erupting all around us. We would run down a street that seemed to have been missed by the bombers and cower for a time in an archway or entrance. But soon flames would shoot up in front of us and multiply like reflections racing toward infinity in a hall of mirrors. Fleeing the intense heat, we tried to move away from what seemed to be the main flight path of the bombers. But often we found the way blocked by a huge crater or hillock of smoldering bricks and flaming wood that had toppled into the street. Sometimes we tried to pick our way over the debris, but then would have to give up and turn back. Everywhere the bellowing wind drove the flames to frenzy, but the larger streets leading from the Alster Lake were the worst. Hot air and gasses flew down these streets with such incredible force that they carried everything that wasn't anchored toward the blazing incinerator that an hour or so earlier had been the districts of Hamm and Hammerbrook.

We found some partial shelter in a basement entrance, but soon that too was ablaze. It was obvious that we couldn't stay where we were; pieces of the building had begun to fall onto the sidewalk. Despite the sustained roar of the wind and the sporadic explosions, I could sometimes hear the great cracking sounds made by the fire. I didn't see how we could avoid being crushed by the collapsing building if we stayed or consumed by flames if we took to the street. I looked at Mother's face and read that she was also undecided as to whether it would be worse to stay or leave. When there was a pause in the bombing, however, she wordlessly wrapped me like a mummy in my blanket. I could hardly breathe and coughed miserably as she picked me up and covered both of us with her blanket. Carrying me in her arms she edged back into the street. By sticking close to building walls and taking advantage of every possible windbreak, she managed to get us both to a more sheltered side street.

We were both exhausted—limping, blistered, and bleeding from our ears and noses—when we stumbled into a crater that had some water at the bottom. The crater appeared to be in the small front garden of what until recently had been a handsome brick home with bays and turrets but was now a smoldering shambles. Mother thoroughly dampened her blanket and draped it over us. The terrible explosions seemed to have abated, although hundreds of incendiary bombs had fallen close by, some landing in rubble no more than a dozen yards away. A canister of liquid phosphorous had hit an office building just down the avenue. As the phosphorus burned and dripped its way through floor after floor, it looked like the lights were being turned on by someone descending methodically through the building. Before the phosphorus reached the ground floor, flames were leaping from the windows of the upper floors.

Next I saw a woman carrying an infant come running down the street along the same route we had taken. She was followed by a young man dressed in the khaki shorts and shirt of the Hitler Youth. I thought they must be fleeing from a bomb shelter that had been damaged, possibly the one Mother had been heading for when we first left our apartment building. The woman looked to be about Mother's age. Her dress appeared to have been burned, leaving her almost completely naked below the waist. Despite his agile build and hiking shoes, the boy seemed to be having trouble keeping on his feet. I thought his trouble might be due to the hot wind roaring down the avenue in front of us and almost expected to see him lifted up as he ran. Instead, after passing us at a gallop, he slowed to a grotesque caricature of walking, more like slow-motion skating, one leaden foot moving seconds after the other, with his arms spread out from his sides for balance. It took a while before I realized that both he and the woman were wading in molten asphalt. The woman slipped a couple of times and touched the pavement with one hand but managed to recover. Then she slowly fell head first toward the street, twisting at the last moment so that she landed on her back with the baby on her chest. The boy tried to reach her but slipped and fell, got up and fell again, and then again. Despite the incredible noise, I thought I could hear their screams and ducked down into the crater with my eyes closed and my hands over my ears.

Mother climbed to the edge of the crater and for a moment I feared she was going to dash out to try to save the baby. But the hot wind burned her face and forced her back down. We lay in the crater beneath the blanket, getting hotter and hotter as gale force winds drove the flames into the sky. The image of the woman and the Hitler Youth writhing in hot asphalt remained vivid in the sweltering darkness until I realized that I was gasping for breath like a fish on land. No matter how deeply I inhaled, I couldn't get enough air into my lungs. When it seemed that I was about to suffocate and sink under the dark water, I pulled the blanket away and stuck my head out. Flaming logs and lumber, some of the planks several feet long, were sailing about in the air along with millions and millions of sparks swirling with such speed they seemed to be tiny streaks of light. Without thinking I opened my mouth wide and tried to suck in as much air as I could, until sharp needles of pain in my chest told me this was a big mistake. I slumped back more terrified than ever. When I closed my eyes it felt like we were lying between railroad tracks while an endless train rumbled over us so swiftly that sparks from the wheels prickled my face.

I passed out for a time, awakening to find that breathing was still painful but that the explosions had stopped and the wind, though still almost as hot as steam, was not as strong. The heat was intense but so was our thirst, and we couldn't remain in the crater any longer without trying to drink the stinking water in the bottom. When we emerged we seemed to be in a winter snowstorm, with white flakes of ash flying in the wind. They looked so cool that I wanted to stick out my tongue to taste them, but there was still enough fire left in them to burn painfully. Mother wrapped us both in her blanket and we tried to walk so that the hot ashes were not blowing directly at us.

We hadn't progressed very far when we began to see bodies. Before leaving the area of the crater, Mother had cautiously confirmed that the woman and her child and the Hitler Youth were dead, but she had shielded me from the sight. Although earlier we hadn't seen many other people in the streets, after the raid they seemed to be everywhere. Some, the obvious victims of exploding bombs, had been terribly torn or dismembered. Fire or heat had killed many more. Most were lying face down. The flames had shorn their hair and clothes, seared and swollen their buttocks, split their skin and raised their hips a few inches off the ground. Though unmistakably human, they looked like huge bratwursts. The smell of burned flesh churned our stomachs and made us want to cry, but we hadn't enough water in us for tears or throwing up. Instead, I clasped Mother and buried my face in her dress.

Desperate for something to drink we headed toward the Eilbeck Canal. Although we couldn't have been more than six or seven blocks away, it took another hour to make our way to an underpass near a wide part of the canal. Hundreds of people were in the water, most of them near the opposite shore, where the water was shallow, much shallower than usual because of the lack of rain in the past few months. Even more were on the banks, quite a few of them obviously dead. Some had faces as swollen and red as Chinese lanterns: their heads had been cooked while their bodies had been under water. Piteous moans, whimpering, and cries of anguish rose from the canal. The screams of children seemed to hang in the air like paper kites. Now and then someone on the shore would start shrieking and jumping about and then leap into the water.

Near our apartment building, one of the 45,000 people killed by the firestorm.

Normally, Hamburgers were extremely stoic. Sometimes they might mutter curses or shout insults, but typically they clamped their jaws and grimly endured adversity in silence. That morning, however, they voiced their pain.

Listening to the voices emanating from the water, I realized that many had been burned by the phosphorous. Just as it burned through the floors of a building, it quickly penetrated living flesh and bone. Judging from the grotesque shapes and expressions of the dead, many had died in agony. Those still in the canal had discovered that the phosphorus became inactive when it was submerged, but if they left the water, it would start burning again as fiercely as before.

When another series of air-raid alarms announced that more bombers were within thirty minutes of Hamburg, a spontaneous wailing and cursing arose from the sufferers, and then quickly subsided as if the effort had been too taxing or embarrassing. A few people started moving toward the church, whether to pray or take shelter in the basement, I couldn't say. Most, like us, remained by the canal. At the second alarm, which signaled the arrival of bombers within fifteen minutes, Mother recovered our blanket and wet it again in the canal. We were sitting with our feet in the water when the final alarm announced that the bombers were overhead. The unexpected quickness of their arrival gave us hope. If the bombers were moving so much faster than expected, they were probably the smaller British Mosquitoes rather than Lancasters or American Flying Fortresses returning to pulverize whatever was still standing. We lay on the bank for roughly two hours, listening to an occasional Mosquito Bomber buzz across the sky to drop a few more bombs into the billowing smoke.

Long before the all-clear sounded, Mother and I began to have stomach cramps and to vomit the canal water we had drunk earlier. On our way toward St. Gertrude Church in search of fresh water, I stumbled over the outstretched arm of a woman lying in the grass

A view of our residential district (Eilbeck) after the streets were cleared of rubble. (Source: Imperial War Museum)

presumably dead. But she wasn't. She suddenly rose up to a sitting position and cried out, "Oh, God! Oh, dear God!"

Terribly upset, I said I was sorry and apologized for hurting her.

She replied that I hadn't hurt her and asked me to help her to get up. She also asked if it was still dark.

As I helped her up, I told her it was only a little past noon, but so dark from smoke and clouds that I hadn't seen her.

The woman looked to be a few years younger than Mother and quite a bit plumper, with the kind of figure that men often called "juicy." Her dress was wrinkled and damp and dirty, apparently from being in the canal, and long strands of blond hair streaked down her face, which was red and blistered. She kept her eyes shut and held her hands up to keep her balance. A gold cross lay just below the base of her neck and a red and white pin with a black swastika in its center was attached to her dress over her heart.

"Let me help you," Mother said, taking the woman by the elbows to steady her.

The woman thanked her and said that she couldn't see very well, having injured her eyes while in the canal to escape the heat. Mother offered to take her to St. Gertrude's Church, which was only about fifty meters away, telling her that someone there would be able to help her.

But a bossy churchwoman insisted that the injured woman needed to go at once to a women's clinic several blocks away, in the Barmbeck district. Mother offered to guide her if she felt able to walk through the rubble-strewn streets.

The woman said she lived in Barmbeck and thought she could walk to the clinic if she had some shoes, having lost hers in the canal. The bossy woman found shoes—I felt certain she took them from a dead woman—and stuffed them with bits of rag to make them fit. Then we set off, Mother taking one hand of the woman, who said her name was Maria, and me taking the other.

Hundreds of dazed and injured women and children, many of them also burn victims, coughed and wept in the haze surrounding the small women's clinic in the Barmbeck district. We couldn't get Maria inside or find anyone who would take her off our hands. Everyone was exhausted or in pain or both. We waited with Maria in the gathering darkness, trying to recover some strength and to figure out what to do next. A woman wearing a Red Cross bandana, who was circulating among the injured, eventually stopped to ask about Maria, who couldn't see anything and felt terrible when she tried. The Red Cross woman promised Maria that she would get better in time but said that the clinic couldn't do anything for her now. She told Maria to rest, to keep her eyes clean and to get to a hospital or come back tomorrow or the next day if possible. We walked her home and put her to bed. She lived in a basement apartment that was mercifully cooler and less smoky than the world outside, and she didn't have to ask us to stay the night; when the air-raid sirens resumed their wailing, we lay down, she in her bed and Mother and I on her couch, too tired and shaken to do anything more.

The next day, while I prepared something for all of us to eat, Mother went into the streets early to look for water. She wore one of Maria's dresses and, at Maria's urging, took her ration card and some money. I feared for her, but she returned about an hour later with bottled water and good news, both of which she had obtained from a friendly fire warden at Karstadt Department Store. He told her that the firestorm had consumed our district and several others but had stopped short of Brandsende. Like other elderly wardens he took pride in Hamburg's history, and he was so pleased that Mother had asked about Brandsende that he sold her some water from the emergency reserve earmarked for the store's two large air-raid shelters. Otherwise, there was no bottled water to be had.

Mother also reported that Maria's Barmbeck area was still relatively unscathed but that thousands of people from all areas were in the streets trying to get out of Hamburg. Word had spread that the British intended to level the entire city. Maria said she had heard rumors of uprisings by slave laborers and prisoners of war at some of the many compounds in and near the city. Mother said she hadn't heard of such developments and that as far as she knew prisoners were still helping with rescue operations.

There were several more air-raid alarms during the day and the early part of the night, but the exodus of people continued without letup. When the seventh alarm sounded shortly before midnight, Mother and Maria talked briefly about trying to get to a shelter. We stayed because the basement was as secure as some shelters and a lot more comfortable and convenient. Also, there was no electricity and hence no radio confirmation that the British were coming again in great numbers. Soon after the attack began we realized that they had targeted Barmbeck. Mother and I climbed into bed with Maria, who trembled and clung to Mother more forcefully than I did. Except for the fact that I didn't feel nearly as exposed and we weren't forced into the streets, it was a repeat of our previous horror. An explosion caused the roof and top floors of our small building to collapse, filling the front and back entrances to our cellar with debris. There was a strong smell of spilled kerosene and from time to time ceiling beams and bricks crashed down. Afraid to move and barely able to breathe, we recovered our wits sufficiently to roll out of and then under the bed.

Perhaps because it was necessary to talk to keep from going insane, Mother revealed to Maria that she was sharing her misery with Jews.

"You should have told me!" Maria said after a pause. "I wish you had told me!"

Choking back sobs she went on to explain that she was in love with a married man who was a Jew. They had worked at the same bank in Berlin and had continued to see one another after he had been fired and after her family and friends had in effect excommunicated her. Before the outbreak of war, they had broken off the affair and he had fled with his wife and child to England. The last time they were together, he had made her promise that she would move to Hamburg and join the Nazi party to rid herself of the stain of their affair and secure the protection she would need as a single woman without family.

Mother told Maria that she understood that people sometimes needed to wear a disguise. She said that her husband was totally against the war but had gone into the Luftwaffe so that she and their daughters might live. Hours later three weary men wearing soiled prison stripes finally pulled us out of the rubble. Before Maria was led away to receive medical aid, I noticed that she had quietly jettisoned her swastika pin.

Where could we go? We were told that we couldn't get to Brandsende because soldiers had cordoned off the streets near City Hall. A rescue worker told us to go to the Stadtpark. There we would at least be safe from the fires, and we could try to get transportation out of the city. On the way we saw that the Karstadt Department Store had collapsed onto its two air-raid shelters. People who were disinterred from the shelter reserved for store employees and city officials were dazed but unhurt, but rescue workers had taken hundreds of dead women and children from the other shelter and were bringing out more as we passed. Mother squeezed my hand to signal her relief that we had not been in the shelter of the dead.

There were thousands of desperate refugees in the park by the time we got there. Many looked extremely angry, others glanced about with blank faces, seemingly unable to get their bearings, while a few grinned so foolishly I thought they must have lost their minds. Police and other city officials were loading people into every type of vehicle and sending them off without much inquiry into who was going where. Baby buggies and other paraphernalia were left standing where they had been left; abandoned pets chased one another through the park.

Five days after the firestorm, my father's written notice about a found family and his request for news of his lost family.

I didn't think that Mother had decided to leave the city, but when a policeman herded us toward the back of a truck with a canvas cover she didn't pull back or resist. The truck driver demanded some money and answered her question as to where he was going with a single word: "South!" And so we left the city. British fighters were reported to have strafed columns of fleeing refugees, and we stayed off the road the next day, parked in an orchard under trees laden with unripe apples to which we helped ourselves. I found swallowing painful but the tart flavor was heavenly. Mother and I took as many apples as we could carry and still had some when we were dumped in the Bavarian village of Hof at around two in the morning. I was more asleep than awake as arrangements were made to sleep in a room over a tavern beside a trout stream.

I can't remember much of the next few days other than the pain that came with eating and breathing. As I recovered I began to appreciate the fact that the bombing had not taken our lives but had kept us from being deported. Although it had been an incredible horror, we had emerged whole and seemingly safe, at least for now. Daily I gained strength and inner happiness from the knowledge that my mother was my savior, my beautiful hero. She had outwitted the Gestapo and faced down the police and the Nazis in the shelter. She had held my hand and led me through the exploding streets; she had never let go.

Chapter 6

The Moon in Hiding

One morning while I was recuperating in Hof there was news from my father. Mother told me she had talked with him by telephone. He had arrived in Hamburg the day after our building had been bombed and had stayed at Cousin Inge's on Brandsende. He had written a message for us on the wall of our apartment building while the corpses of neighbors lay nearby. Though the British had made another massive raid on the city, Rena, Inge, and her family had survived the bombs. A day or so after the phone call Inge arrived in Hof with Rena and told us that Father had arranged for us to take refuge on the farm of Marie Pimber, the woman who had been taking care of my other sister, Helga.

Frau Pimber was part of a small network of people, almost all communists or former communists, whom Father had called upon for assistance of one sort or another. But not all of those who risked their lives to oppose the Nazis were willing to assist Jews; some were as anti-Semitic as the next German. Unsure of Frau Pimber's feelings on this subject, Father had told her that blond-haired, fair-skinned Helga was his daughter, but not that he was married to a Jew. He had encouraged Frau Pimber to present Helga to the local community and authorities as a Christian evacuee from the bombings. Many thousands of children had been sent with government encouragement to live in the countryside with relatives or friends, so there was no reason for anyone to question the arrangement. Helga was in effect hiding in the open, living almost as a member of Frau Pimber's family.

When he asked Frau Pimber to hide Mother, Rena, and me, Father had told her we were his family and that we were Jews, which meant that our presence had to be a complete secret from everyone else, including Helga. Frau Pimber didn't much like the idea of hiding Jews, an offense that could get her killed, but she had been childless until Helga arrived and she had become so attached that she thought of Helga as her own. Faced with the choice of losing Helga or letting us live on her farm, and offered as much material support as Father could muster, Frau Pimber agreed. Mother was relieved, but we were not at all certain what would be in store for us when we reached the Pimber farm.

I still had not recovered from what Mother and a man in Hof had called smoke poisoning and was more asleep than awake when we arrived after midnight on a cool morning in late August. Mother carried a lantern and the truck driver carried me to a place to sleep. It was impossible to see anything of my surroundings and I didn't have the energy to try, but I had the uneasy feeling as I lost consciousness again that I was being buried alive instead of being put to bed.

I awoke hours later lying on a ledge in a dugout or cellar with an earthen ceiling only a foot or so above my head. A woman with a large, pink face wrapped in a black shawl held a lantern and glared at me with eyes as hard and shiny as chestnuts. When I began to cough, she squinted and bared large, stained, forward-slanting teeth as if she would bite me unless I stopped at once. From the darkness I heard my mother's reassuring voice: "Don't worry, darling; we are safe, now. Frau Pimber has a nice place where she is going to let us stay." There was a snort as the bulky woman withdrew, leaving us in the grave-like darkness. Although the dirt roof was too low for

Mother to stand erect, she gave me water from a metal cup and stroked my cheeks and forehead until I stopped coughing and fell back to sleep.

The earthen dugout, I soon learned, was not our primary shelter. A few days after we arrived, we moved into a small shed secluded among oaks and pines, a short dash from the hazelnut bushes that concealed the entrance to the dugout. Covered with tarpaper, the shed had been a place for tools and winter plants, but it was outfitted with a small stove, two cots, one of which I shared with Rena although she preferred to sleep with Mother, a small table, a chair, and a single electric light. We were to stay in the dugout only when visitors came to the farm or when a neighbor, a minor Nazi official, spent holidays or weekends at his country house nearby. Marie Pimber would shut off our electricity to let us know when we had to move into the dugout. Fortunately, the *Unterfuhrer's* duties in what was left of Hamburg didn't allow him to visit his farm often.

Frau Pimber was as wide as a cow and even more imposing, at least to me. Although I didn't know why, I knew from the first that she disliked me, and I did my best to avoid getting caught in the glare of her perpetually squinting eyes. When she opened her great jaws I was repelled by the guttural harshness of her voice as well as the hideous teeth. Hiding behind a bush or tree I agonized as she bullied my mother. She never let Mother forget that we would have been killed if she hadn't agreed to hide us. For every potato, every turnip, she exacted a price in hard labor. With Mother's agreement, she told Helga that we had fled to Switzerland and didn't allow Helga to come anywhere near us, perhaps telling her that the people who lived in the woods were evil and would kidnap and kill or sell her if they got the chance. Such stories were told routinely to rural children and wouldn't raise an eyebrow if repeated. Occasionally I would see Helga's platinum mop from a distance and feel an almost overpowering urge to approach her and tell her the truth. A natural tomboy and only a year and a half younger, Helga had been my true

Mother peeks out of our hideaway at Frau Pimber's farm.

best friend and natural playmate. But I knew that it was safer for her and for us if our lives were kept separate. I also understood that Helga was Frau Pimber's hostage and that there was no telling what Frau Pimber would do if the arrangement was disturbed in any way. She might even denounce us.

When Frau Pimber wasn't around I was profoundly thankful for our refuge from the Gestapo. Like everyone else, I knew that Jewish children were being deported to the camps to be killed. After she stopped pretending to be my friend, seven-year-old Monika had taunted me with the threat to have me sent "up the chimney," meaning sent to a camp to be killed and cremated. Some adults might survive at least for a time as slave laborers, but not the children. I was also grateful to be away from the bombs and the flames. Sometimes, when we had to hide in the dugout, my body would tense and shake as scenes from the bombings silently projected themselves against the utter darkness. Then, and in my dreams, I would see a fireman climb a ladder toward people frantically waving from an upper window of a burning building, and would try to will an ending other than the collapse of the wall into flames. I also saw the baked gingerbread faces of the people who had turned us away from their bunker or the wildly gyrating bodies of people who had been hit by burning phosphorous.

Such images slowly faded and were sometimes replaced by the distinctive features of an owl, which I willed myself to see in the darkness, having seen the living creature one evening in the branches of a tree. The owl had stared at me and looked fierce, but not threatening, rather as if it would pounce on anything that might try to harm me, such as one of the field mice that sometimes gnawed its way into our shack. I often looked for the owl in the trees and sometimes saw it again, flying from one perch to another or standing majestically in the tree. More often I would hear it calling— *whooo . . . whooo . . . whooo.* Lying in bed, I would concentrate on the image and voice of the owl to take my mind off my hunger.

Hunger was constant and often acute. It was so persistent and compelling that much of the time it was difficult to focus on other things. Although we were in the country, the Pimbers' main crops were hay and wheat, which they sold. They had a small vegetable garden, which Mother weeded and tended, but we were forbidden to take anything unless it was given to us by Frau Pimber's own hand. So there were many days when we had nothing to eat. A rare feast would be a couple of potatoes, boiled in their jackets so as not to lose a single bit of nourishment. Turnips were more plentiful, and I gratefully accepted when Mother, pretending she couldn't stand them, gave me part of her portion. She was not only my savior, she was also my teacher, my comforter, my companion, and I loved her and desperately wanted her to be happier. I couldn't bear it when she was depressed.

Although Mother possessed seemingly unshakable composure, both of us stopped breathing one autumn morning when there was a heavy knocking on the door of our hut. We knew it wasn't Frau Pimber, because she never bothered to knock. When the banging persisted, Mother finally opened the door to a woman who was even larger and more ungainly than Frau Pimber. She looked bewildered and her watery blue eyes substantially widened when she entered holding two eggs in her outstretched hand. She continued to look startled and the flesh beneath her chin quivered as she told us that she was Liese, Frau Pimber's neighbor and oldest friend.

"Don't be afraid," she said, "I won't tell anyone. I have known since you first came. You have nothing to fear from me; I wouldn't harm a living thing. Not a thing!"

After a pause Mother introduced herself. The contrast between the two women was overwhelming. Despite all she had been through, Mother looked as refined and beautiful as a photo in a fashion magazine. The naked light that hung above our table lengthened her lashes and dramatically shaded the high, soft line of her cheeks. Although her large, dark eyes no longer sparkled, sorrow had left a glow inside them that made mine grow moist as I looked at her. Even her damaged and repaired clothes looked smart, while our fleshy visitor resembled a random pile of rather worn laundry. Simple country kindness signed the woman's coarse features, however, and gave her voice reassuring warmth. She embraced us and kissed Rena. Afterwards we always referred to her as if she were an adored aunt, calling her Tante Lieschen.

This unexpected visit and the one that followed a few days later made me want to explore the outer limits of our earthy confinement. Although I fully understood the reasons for Mother's absolute rule against leaving our tiny perimeter, when she was working for Frau Pimber I began to stray beyond the woods, looking for flowers in the grain field along the road. I was drawn inexorably toward the Nazi official's house. Peering through a bit of hedge along the fence line that separated his property from the Pimbers', I saw no signs of life. But I did see an apple tree laden with large, red-tinged fruit, which stood not far away, just behind the wire fence. My stomach tied itself into knots while I imagined myself tearing into two tart beauties at once and then taking a skirt-full home to Mother. But I didn't dare. I went home ravaged by hunger and anxiety. I knew that I couldn't tell Mother I had gone so close to the Nazi's house, but at the same time I imagined that she might be so glad to have some apples that she would forgive me for disobeying her if I managed to take some.

Inevitably I returned to the tree. On the third visit I crawled on all fours close enough to see that there were plenty of apples on the ground just waiting to be carried away. I also saw that one heavily laden branch drooped low enough for me to reach some apples if I climbed up the fence. The longer I considered it the more confident I became. Finally I climbed, careful not to tear my dress on the barbed wire, then reached up and grabbed first one and then a second plump apple. I took a large bite, savoring the juicy flesh, and then another before looking down.

My triumph quickly turned into terror. A man wearing a felt hat and a forest green jacket was marching toward me from the house, his jaw thrust forward angrily. Almost reflexively, I tried to cover the place on my dress where the Star of David would have been if I had been wearing one. The silly gesture made me wobble on the fence and then lose my balance completely. Falling backward I hit the ground hard enough to knock the air from my lungs and lay gasping, certain that the furious Nazi would soon lay his hands on me. After what seemed like an eternity I managed to rise, retrieve the apples, and run into the woods, where I hid behind a tree until I was confident that I wasn't being pursued. I tried to eat one of the apples but couldn't. I hid them and returned to our hut, my heart pounding at the thought of facing Mother. I knew I had betrayed us, and I expected the SS to arrive at any moment with dogs and guns. When Mother asked where I had been and why I looked so pale, guilt exploded inside my chest, but I bit my lip and kept silent.

That night I dreamed that I found a baby lying in rubble, its blanket smoldering and beginning to flame. I wanted to save it, but a helmeted fireman with an axe in his hand chased me away. Everywhere I turned there was a wall and in every window there was a face ringed with fire. Waking up I saw for an instant the sharp face of the Nazi staring at me. Eventually I went back to sleep, but for many mornings I awoke to the thought that, because of me, soldiers and police with dogs might arrive at any moment to arrest us.

During one visit Tante Lieschen told us that, although she and Marie Pimber had been friends since childhood, they had never agreed about Communism or Nazism. Tante Lieschen had refused to believe that Hitler was an evil leader. We were the first Jews she had ever known. But since becoming our friend, she found it impossible to reconcile her go-along politics with our plight. She now realized how shameful it was to persecute Jews. But when she had told her old friend about her change of heart, Frau Pimber had become furious and had forbidden her to visit us or send us food. After that, Tante Lieschen came rarely and only at dusk. Even then she rarely escaped Frau Pimber's increasingly malicious eye.

On my ninth birthday, Tante Lieschen surprised us with the ingredients for a cake. It was my birthday present and would be our first cake in years. While it was baking we inhaled the scent and devoured each crumb a hundred times over in our imagination. When at last it was finished, however, we discovered that Mother had somehow confused the contraband sugar with salt and had put the salt in the batter. The cake looked perfect, but was nauseating. When I tried to eat it anyway, Mother wept as if someone had died.

Tante Lieschen also loaned us a radio. A few days later, while I stood guard outside our hut as Mother listened to the BBC, I heard and then saw Frau Pimber calling her cat, a beautiful smoky-blue Persian that had been given to her by Tante Lieschen. The cat soon came and Frau Pimber grabbed it up in her arms. But instead of caressing it, she put it into a cloth sack, causing the cat to howl eerily. While I wondered what was going on, Frau Pimber added a rock to the sack, tied it shut with a length of clothesline and carried it to the well between our shed and her house. For a moment she held the writhing bag in front of her, and then dropped it down the well.

I jumped up and started toward the well but, sensing danger and remembering that I had to get back to my post as Mother's sentinel, I quickly slumped to the ground. After what seemed an interminable period, Frau Pimber hauled up the line and lifted the dripping but unmoving sack from the well. It was then that she looked in my direction. She made an evil grimace, untied the line and dragged the sack up the hill to her house.

Later that day I saw Frau Pimber coming toward our shed. I put my head in the door and alerted Mother, then ran to the dugout. While the two women were talking, I went to the well and looked into its cool and silent depths. I needed to make some sense out of what I had seen, to give it another interpretation or a different outcome. But staring into the well thinking about what I had seen made me feel worse.

As I rose up and turned to leave, Frau Pimber's hand flew against my face. She hit me with such force that I was knocked against the stone facing of the well. Too startled to cry out, I ran away as fast as I could, feeling that if I didn't escape I would experience the same fate as the cat. I raced toward our shack, holding my flaming cheek in my hand, wanting desperately to be comforted by Mother. When I reached the door, however, I stopped and tried to compose myself, not wanting to upset Mother too greatly, fearing that she might try to do something rash, and feeling vaguely guilty, as if I had done something to provoke Frau Pimber. As I stood there gulping air, I touched the back of my head, which had begun to sting a little where it had hit the wall. My fingertip felt slightly wet, and I soon saw that I had bled a bit, not much but enough to make Mother wildly angry. So I turned and ran away from our shack and into the woods.

I ran through the trees until I came to a broad ditch, which I leapt going full tilt, landing at the edge of a narrow dirt lane. I scurried across the road even though I knew this was strictly forbidden and plunged into the field of green and golden wheat on the other side. I ran low through stalks almost as high as my head until I felt sure that I couldn't be seen from the road. Then I stopped and caught my breath and looked about me. The wheat seemed to be moving and I could hear it rustling, so that for several seconds I thought I was being pursued, but it was merely the wind caressing the bristling stalks. The sky was so full of light that it was like a dazzling smile that entreated me to smile back despite my fears and the sting on the back of my head. My lips opened and widened when a blood-red poppy caught my eye. As I watched it nod and sway gracefully in the breeze, all thoughts of the recent unpleasantness evaporated.

I crept toward the poppy as if it were a bird that might fly away. Then I lovingly examined its exquisitely simple features. Four crimson, fan-shaped outer leaves casually overlapped, cupping a pale green pod set beneath a miniature shower of gold-tipped stamen. After I had admired it from every angle, noticing also that a black design in the bottom of the cup blurred to purple, I plucked the entire flower, cutting the stem low so as to include all the green buds. Then I looked around for more.

The field that had looked from the road like rippling cloth of gold was stippled with softly glowing poppies and dark blue cornflowers, while countless white-petaled daisies serenely beamed yellow faces back at the sun. How wonderful, I thought. Marguerites are Mother's namesake flower, the cornflowers match Rena's eyes, and I adore poppies like nothing else. But after I had gathered an overwhelming armful, I realized that, as had been the case with the stolen apples, I could not take the flowers home with me. Mother would know that I had crossed the road into the field and my flowers therefore would give her pain rather than pleasure. Even though the Americans and English had landed armies in France and the Russians were furiously punishing the German armies in the East, giving us genuine hope that the war would not go on forever, I knew that we could not take any chances.

Standing with the flowers at the edge of the field, I was so disappointed that I wanted to cry. Instead I turned and walked back among the golden fuzzy stalks, stopping when I reached what I judged to be the center of the field. There I lay down my flowers, arranging them in a circular pattern, and went to pluck more. I heaped these upon the others and kept collecting until I had gathered enough to make a thick, soft pallet. Then I lay down on my bed of flowers and looked up at the sky.

I watched the platinum sun move like a shuttle through layers of fleece. Beneath the clouds a flock of birds wheeled and soared and changed directions in a flash, repeating their acrobatics in every quarter of the sky before plunging into a corner of the wheat field. I forgot that I was hungry, forgot the flames and screams and Marie Pimber's cat, even forgot that Mother would be listening to the BBC and worrying because I was not there. I closed my eyes but didn't make pictures in my mind as I usually did while lying in bed or in our earthen dugout. I didn't want anything to interfere with the beauty of the moment and the wonderful feeling of solitary freedom. Listening to my own heartbeat, the rustling wheat, and the strange pulsing sounds of insects, I must have fallen into a light sleep.

Suddenly a large, rough hand covered my mouth and most of my face. A man's voice, gruff and urgent, was telling me or asking me something over and over in mangled German and some language I couldn't identify. Occasionally, he would loosen his grip on my face so that I could breathe and answer him, but his breath was so bad that it was even more suffocating than his hand. In response I shook my head violently, covering my ears with my hands to indicate that I didn't want to listen to him anymore. Although most of what he said was incomprehensible, something in the center of my being told me that he wanted to know exactly what I must not tell him. My fear was so transparent that my tormentor paused, bent his head closer and kissed both my eyes. When he withdrew his lips I could see that tears were running down his bristly face, streaking the grime in a way that made him look like a sad clown who was trying to laugh. Tears also began to trickle from my eyes.

The man continued to command me but his voice was much gentler, sounding almost as much like a plea as an order. He stood me up so that my head was level with his and looked at me with eyes as blue as the cornflowers but so searching that I closed mine, as if to keep him from reading my thoughts. I understood that he wanted me to take him to Mother, but I couldn't do this because I knew that if she were discovered she would be killed and so would Rena and probably even Helga. At the same time it was clear that the man would not let me go until he got what he wanted, and there was nowhere I could run if I should escape his grasp. Remorse and guilt at the thought that my disobedience might cause Mother's death overwhelmed me. It would be better for me to die here on these flowers, I thought, but I knew that I couldn't make that happen.

The man didn't try to hurt me. Instead he knelt and held me loosely in his arms. I was convinced that he was not German, much less a Nazi. His attempts at speaking German were so clumsy that it was easy to pretend I couldn't understand him. He was bony and wretched and filthy looking and I was fairly certain that he had been a prisoner although I couldn't tell what kind. Beneath the grime and whiskers his skin was pale and the close-cropped hair on his head and the hair on his hands and wrists looked reddish-blond. I didn't think he was Jewish, but it was clear to me that he had suffered a lot.

I don't know how long the impasse lasted, only that I began to cry again and that the man clasped me firmly in his arms and did his best to reassure me that he meant no harm. I believed him but knew that didn't make it okay for me to betray our hiding place. Eventually, still feeling like I had swallowed fire, I led the man across the road toward our shack.

Mother was standing outside when we approached through the trees. She turned pale and clamped a hand over her mouth to stifle a scream. The man came near and spoke to her earnestly but haltingly in crude German and some other language. Mother didn't say much in reply, but picked me up in her arms and carried me inside, leaving the door open for him to come in behind us.

Mother didn't scold me for leaving the area and leading the man to our hiding place, but she didn't have to. I was ashamed of my behavior and aware that the man's presence increased the possibility that we would be discovered and killed. Although we were undernourished, he was starving, so we shared what food we had. Late at night, he would go foraging for more, but he was not very successful and his efforts increased the risk that we might be discovered. He understood the situation and didn't remain with us for more than a week or so. Despite my lingering shame at having betrayed our hiding place, for the brief time that he was with us, he made me feel that I was very special.

"You saved my life," he would say, looking at me with love in his eyes, repeating the phrase and stroking my hair.

I learned that his name was Carlo and he was from Yugoslavia, a country I hadn't heard much about. He had been arrested after his country had fallen to Germany and had been deported to East Prussia to work in coal mines near the Polish border. When the Red Army began to approach the area, he and other slave laborers were marched west to work on defensive fortifications deeper within Germany. During the march he escaped and began to make his way toward Belgrade, where he had a wife and daughter he hadn't seen in almost three years. Travelling only at night to avoid recapture, he had been hiding in the woods when he saw me dash into the wheat field to gather flowers.

Carlo told Mother and me that he had a daughter my age and that it felt like he was holding her when he put his arms around me. He also said that even as a prisoner in a remote labor camp, he had heard about what the Germans were doing to Jews. When he talked about the cruelty of the Nazis or about his wife and daughter, he would sometimes begin to cry. At such times I would try to comfort him and go close to him so that he could stroke my hair or give me a hug if he liked. Although much thinner and more emotional, Carlo reminded me of Father and helped me to recall things about Father that I seemed almost to have forgotten.

After Carlo left us, I began to think again about the beautiful poppies and cornflowers and daisies and yearned to return to the wheat field. In my mind I often pictured and rearranged the flowers. At night I even dreamed about them. In one dream the flame-like poppies set the field on fire and I ran about trying to put out the flames until I finally collapsed on a bed of flowers that turned out to be water lilies in a still pond. Lying quietly on a huge lily pad in the center of the pond I knew I was safe from the fire. But when I heard voices wafting over the water, I forced myself to wake up.

* * *

On an exceedingly windy evening in early autumn Frau Pimber opened our door, thrust her massive body through the frame, and shouted that a thunderstorm was on the way. She said that Mother and I must help her gather hay and put it in their small barn before it was ruined by rain. Mother insisted that I stay with Rena if there was going to be a storm and followed Frau Pimber out the door. Within a few minutes the storm hit. Lightning flashed and cracked and thunderclaps shook the walls of our shack. Wind stripped the tar paper from our roof, after which hailstones rattled the bare wood like handfuls of hurled pebbles. I rocked Rena in my arms, but after our one light went out she began to wail as loudly as she could and I wished that I could broadcast the sound so that Mother would hear it and come running.

As the thunder and lightning gradually moved on the rain increased in intensity, creating the sensation that we had drifted under a waterfall. Soon I could hear and feel rain coming through the roof in several places. After lighting a lantern I tried to move things around to minimize the damage. But the rain continued to pummel us and the leaks became more numerous and both Rena and I grew more and more miserable. Twice the storm let up for a time until fresh gales roared toward us. I spent the intervals of relative calm in the doorway holding the lantern to help Mother make her way to us as rapidly as possible. When she didn't return, I began to worry about her more and more, imagining all sorts of mishaps that might be keeping her away, including treachery by Frau Pimber.

After what seemed like hours, the wind and rain departed and the dripping stopped inside our house. I put Rena to sleep by telling her a story about a girl who fell into a lake looking at her own reflection in the water but was saved by her sister who gave her a beautiful new dress that she made herself to replace the one that got wet. When Mother still didn't return, I became even more fearful that something might have happened to her and that she might be trapped under a fallen tree or in need of help. At the same time I was certain that even if she was injured she would never forgive me for leaving Rena. I decided to go and look for her anyway.

As I started out an almost full moon escaped the clouds long enough to reveal large puddles ahead. But it didn't stay out long enough to enable me to avoid them. So I sloshed through water almost up to my knees and mud that tried to pull my shoes off my feet. After I had waded to within a few yards of the barn I heard an unexpected but not altogether unfamiliar rustling sound that I couldn't quite identify. Not wanting to stop, I stepped ahead and was surprised and horrified to feel the ground give way entirely. I slid off-balance into a torrent in which I could neither swim nor stand.

Stone fists battered and scraped my body as the current pulled me by my dress through the water, suddenly jerking my head below the surface for terrifying seconds. Although Father had taught me how to swim, nothing could have prepared me for this. Wildly thrashing about, gulping filthy water, and grabbing at everything my hands touched, I was tumbled headlong by the current until I slid to a halt in a shallow stretch of what I then recognized as the barn's drainage ditch, greatly enlarged and coursing with water as never before. Frantically trying to scramble up a steep bank I slid and fell back into the surging current and was swept along several more yards until I became beached again in a shallower passage. I was on my back in the frothing water and too petrified to move when I became aware of the rhythmic *whooing* of the barn owl that I had seen last summer and had listened to in my bed at night. I remembered that the bird's proud but benign way of looking at me had reminded me of my grandmother and I was reassured by its repeated calling, which was like a ship's foghorn giving friendly warning in the darkness. Reassured by the sound of this kindred spirit I recovered my composure and began calmly to feel with my feet for rocks that would hold. Then I reached out until I found roots and rock ledges that I could grip with my hands. Slowly but carefully I clambered out of the enlarged ditch and saw that it was not nearly as deep as it had seemed. Then I stood and listened again for the sound of the owl. Instead, I heard Mother call my name. I ran to her and held her tightly, greatly relieved that we were both okay and reunited again. She practically had to pry me loose so that we could get back to our storm-stricken home where, mercifully, Rena was sound asleep and miraculously dry.

That winter we were colder and hungrier than ever. We had been hiding on Frau Pimber's farm for more than a year, and we were gradually growing thinner and weaker. But we were glad to be away from the bombings and deportations and greatly encouraged by the news that the Russians from the east and the British and Americans from the south were savagely battling their way toward us. Our dream that the war might soon be over was replaced by despair, however, when Frau Pimber came to our shack one evening to report that Father had been arrested. Mother was crushed and so was I at first. But remembering how the Gestapo had treated Uncle Fred, I refused to believe Frau Pimber. Father was too clever and too resourceful to let them catch him, I told myself. I was dying to say as much to Frau Pimber, but refrained, wanting to have as little to do with her as possible, which was difficult because she had begun to listen to news broadcasts at our place. When she told us not long after that Father had been sent to the crumbling Russian front, I felt completely vindicated. "He was too clever for them!" I said to her face. I told her that he could speak Russian and would find a way to join the Russians. This made her snort like an ox, but she didn't contradict me.

As the freezing winter yielded to the fickle rain-and-shine of early spring and the Allied armies bludgeoned their way ever closer, signs of other refugees appeared in the woods near us.

A campfire occasionally flickered in the night and the smells of misery in flight mingled with the heady aroma of pine needles. We began to worry that one or more might invade our hiding place and gradually got used to the idea that sooner or later some sort of encounter was inevitable.

So we were not too surprised on a blustery night in late April when Frau Pimber came to our hut trailing two desperate-looking men, both with bristly beards and both wearing farm clothes apparently supplied by Herr Pimber, who was shorter and thicker than either of them. The taller of the two men limped and carried a crude cane and was much feebler than his younger, relatively robust companion. The latter's eyes swiftly inventoried everything we had, as if to see if anything was worth taking. Despite his apparent good health he looked so haunted and so potentially violent that Mother paled when he asked Rena her name, and my younger sister shyly hid behind Mother and refused to answer.

"Tell him your name," Frau Pimber said. "He won't hurt you."

When Rena remained silent, I decided to answer for her. "Her name's Renate, and she's only five."

Frau Pimber had brought some stale black bread and pale yellow cheese for the men to eat and had even brought portions for us. She said that the men could sleep outside or inside the shack or in the earthen dugout, that it made no difference to her. When Mother tried to say that she would prefer for the men to sleep in the dugout, Frau Pimber cut her short, saying that she knew we had let a man stay with us only a few weeks earlier.

This was the first time she indicated that she had known or found out about Carlo, whose presence we had taken pains to keep secret. Her face was a pink mask shaded by a protruding kerchief so that it was impossible to tell whether she was conveying that she was more observant or more tolerant than we gave her credit for.

After she left, the two men washed their hands and faces and devoured their bread and cheese, as did we. We noticed that the younger one was attentive to his comrade's difficulties and that his ferocious look and manner gradually relaxed, so much so that I felt bold enough to ask him his name.

"Rainer," he said. "My name is Rainer." He tried to smile, but it was obvious that he was out of practice. When I asked where he came from, he said they came from Neuengamme. He asked me if I had heard of Neuengamme.

Like everyone else I knew that Neuengamme was a large concentration camp on the outskirts of Hamburg. But I didn't say so because he looked much too robust to have been a prisoner.

Later the men told Mother that they had fled the camp because all the prisoners were being killed to keep them from telling the Allies, who were expected to arrive in a few days, what had been done to them. When Mother protested that this would mean killing thousands of prisoners, Rainer said that the orders had come from Berlin and were being carried out across Germany. First Mother and then Rena began to cry and I soon joined in, furious also at the two men for bringing such gruesome news. They left the next morning without saying where they were going. I was glad to see them go and told myself they must have been lying.

A few mornings later, as I traced with my finger the lacy shadows cast by new leaves on the wall of our shack, Tante Lieschen sailed up the pathway, skirts and sleeves flying, looking as merry as if she had been sampling schnapps. She stood, smiling and shielding her eyes from the sun while I explained that Mother had taken Rena to look for wild mushrooms in the woods. She took my hand in hers and announced that we would also go for a walk. I wasn't sure what to make of that since I felt certain that she knew I was still not allowed to leave the perimeter. Guessing that we would go looking for Mother or stay within the approved area, I let her lead me. But instead of going in the direction that Mother had taken, Tante Lieschen headed us toward the lane that bordered the woods and the wheat field. Deciding that she must be joking and would soon stop and turn back, I went along with her. When she didn't stop I signaled my unease by dragging my feet until we halted in the shadow of a tree with new, light green leaves.

"It's May Day!" Tante Lieschen piped in a high-pitched voice that came from several feet above my head. "It's May Day and we must gather a lovely bouquet."

I knew that Tante Lieschen liked me and I was glad that she wanted my company. Instead of remembering the near disaster when I had tried to steal apples, I recalled the beauty of the flowers in the wheat field. I inhaled deeply, savoring the mysterious smell of new life, and looked up at huge clouds drifting like icebergs in the cerulean sky. I stopped dragging my feet and went forward eagerly into light so golden I wanted to run my fingers through it. At the sight of wildflowers, I lost all restraint and began to pull the overblown woman along the road after me. It was like towing a massive balloon against the wind and I felt lighter than air as she wagged her kerchiefed head from side to side and laughed.

After gathering handfuls of narcissus near the ruins of a brick farmhouse, we returned to the lane and resumed our mock promenade. Then just ahead of us, Frau Pimber seemed to materialize out of the ground like the devil in a puppet show. But her broad back was to us and I thought with some relief that she hadn't seen us. Suddenly, without looking back, she stopped, bent all the way over, lifted her long, full skirt, pulled down her pink bloomers, and bared her enormous white buttocks. She stayed that way without moving—her large, incredibly pale, unbelievably luminous moon beaming in our faces.

Tante Lieschen stopped and gasped but I stared, enthralled, until she covered my eyes with her own voluminous skirts. I struggled to break free but Tante Lieschen turned me around and walked me back to our hut without allowing me a backward glance.

Mother was so excited by an announcement she had just heard on the radio that, for once, she didn't even ask me where I had been. "Hitler is dead!" she shouted, unable to contain herself. "The beast is dead! The Russians killed him in Berlin. It's over! He's dead! It's over!"

I hugged her and kissed her and danced around the hut while she kissed Rena and threw her into the air and laughed and cried at the same time. I wanted to go outside and shout at the top of my voice, "Hitler is dead! He's dead! He's dead!"

"Are they sure?" Tante Lieschen asked, looking stunned and even a bit sad.

She didn't mean it to be, but her question was a reminder that we weren't yet free. We were still Jews and this was still Germany. The radio hadn't said anything about surrender. But I was so glad that the leader of the haters was dead that I even smiled at Frau Pimber when she came to see what all the ruckus was about. After what I had seen of the ungainly Frau's glistening bottom a short time earlier, I couldn't have kept from smiling at her, even if the news had not been so momentous. I knew that she didn't like me and probably didn't like any Jews, but she was joyful because she disliked Hitler so much, and so did I.

Still smarting from Frau Pimber's moon, Tante Lieschen refused to talk to her former friend except to mutter, when Frau Pimber left to fetch some schnapps, that it was not right to celebrate anyone's death. This provoked an exceptionally loud snort from Frau Pimber, who shot me such a wicked smile as she departed that I thought she might hoist her skirts again. But as if aware that she was denying me a treat, she merely flounced them a bit as she waddled up the path.

* * *

The next day British tanks rumbled over Hamburg's Elbe River bridges and tight-lipped Tommies in olive drab took over the ruined city without a fight. They were greeted like poor relations—or members of an inferior soccer team that had scored a lucky goal—by swaggering Nazis wearing patronizing smiles, belted leather coats, leather boots and rakish, leather-billed garrison caps decorated with death's heads and silver eagles that soared. I was so eager to welcome our liberators that I finally persuaded Mother to take me with her to Hamburg a few days later when she hitched a ride on the back of a farm cart carrying a few metal containers of milk into the city. We had received no word from Father since he had been transferred to the eastern front, and Mother was desperate for news of him and to find out if any relatives who had been sent to concentration camps were still alive.

As the lean but heavily harnessed horse ignored the driver's frequent clucking and slaps with the reins, I imagined being warmly embraced by a ruddy British sergeant-major who would insist on loading the cart with the finest produce from a fancy grocery store. He would then boot the Nazis out of one of the spacious houses that had been taken from Jews and would invite us to move in. When we reached the edge of the city, however, my fantasies were chastened by a landscape more devastated than I could have imagined despite having been present at its destruction. Even the horse was so upset that it whinnied, balked, rolled its eyes, flared its nostrils and refused to enter the canyon of rubble.

With the driver leading the horse, we were jolted through several square miles of residential housing reduced to roofless shells. In time we came to Hasselbrook Strasse, the once lovely street where we had lived in Eilbeck, now abandoned except for a few crows and magpies perched on broken walls or poking in the rubble. I shuddered, recalling the sight of charred bodies lying in the street. Nevertheless I wanted to examine the remains of our building, but Mother stared straight ahead as we passed.

A few blocks past Hasselbrook Strasse, a helmeted Tommy in the turret of a tank halted us and made the cart driver uncover the milk cans before letting us proceed. From time to time we saw other clumps of British soldiers standing, sitting or squatting near tanks

A view of Hasselbrook Street after the bombing.

or armored cars. Many were eating, sometimes beside a campfire in the street. I waved at them and called out hello but they ignored us, barely even looking up from their tankards of tea.

We were stopped again as we approached the main train station. While two helmeted Tommies lifted the lids on the milk canisters, I noticed a tall, rather stout British soldier standing beside a jeep near the station entrance, which was partially blocked by a collapsed section of sheet metal that sloped gracefully to the ground like a sculptured waterfall. His weapon was casually pointed at the ground and he was wearing a smart military shirt and a brown beret with a ribbon trailing from it, reminding me of Uncle Fred in Scottish gear. The soldier seemed to be looking straight at me and smiling as if he knew me. Deciding that he was the one I would thank for my liberation, I jumped off the cart and started toward him, excitedly hopping and skipping in anticipation of greeting and embracing my hero. Before I had gone more than a few yards, however, I saw the muzzle of his weapon rise to the level of my eye, so that I was literally looking down the barrel. *Bam! Bam! Bam!* I saw fire flash from the gun's muzzle and thought I heard the whir of bullets passing overhead.

I dropped to the ground and lay flat, listening to Mother's screams, relieved that they were screams of outrage rather than injury. Then, realizing that she must be running toward me, I scrambled backwards on hands and knees until we collided. Holding hands but crouching low we ran in the opposite direction of the trigger-happy Tommy, toward Cousin Inge's apartment on Brandsende.

True to its name Brandsende and the streets near it had somehow escaped the wrath of the fire bombings. High explosive bombs had wrecked a building or two, but most had landed several blocks away, so that the neighborhood stood out from its surroundings like an urban island in a sea of ruins. Cousin Inge also looked relatively untouched by the horrors she had lived through. She was tall and slender with soft curves, dark blond curls and a spark of mischief in her light blue eyes that reminded me of Father. She even had recent news of Father. She told us he had been captured by the Red Army and was being held in a makeshift prisoner-of-war compound on the Elbe some two hundred kilometers from Hamburg. We were greatly relieved that he was out of the fighting, which continued despite the death of Hitler and the capitulation of Hamburg and Berlin. We also learned that two days earlier thousands of prisoners from the Neuengamme camp had been drowned near Lubeck, having been forced onto ships which the Royal Air Force obligingly bombed and sank.

Within a month after Germany's surrender, Father arrived at Frau Pimber's and I was able to leave her farm forever after almost two years. But burly Frau Pimber didn't give up Helga without a fight. She chased Father around her kitchen table with a butcher knife, furious at him for wanting to take back the beautiful child that she had taken care of for almost four years. Helga was also upset and at one point I feared Mother was going to let Pimber keep her. Before we left Mother thanked Frau Pimber for sheltering us, and both my parents urged me to do the same. But I couldn't. Tante Lieschen laughed and blubbered when I kissed her goodbye. Mother returned the radio to our friend and spoke with feeling about the many kindnesses that she had bestowed, including "the lovely gift of white narcissus."

My parents spent the next few months in Hamburg examining official and unofficial lists of survivors, haunting train stations when refugees arrived, and occasionally dashing through one or more of the occupation zones of the victorious armies in vain attempts to find other members of the family. Father volunteered to help the British relocate refugees or displaced persons, pointing out that he was fluent in several languages and familiar with the cultures and countries from which many of the refugees had come. But a pudding-faced British officer told him that he couldn't possibly be of any assistance to His Majesty's Government, because he was married to a Jew.

Father went into the business of erecting Quonset or Nissen huts as shelters for the many thousands of people who were without homes. Mother helped with this enterprise, but she continued privately to help people link up with living relatives. There were many reports of the reappearance of people given up for dead, but almost all were Gentiles. Only a hundred or so Jews were still alive in Hamburg; some 17,000 had been killed or had fled. Among the last to die were several Jewish girls who had been used for medical experiments. They were hanged in a Hamburg school when the British reached the outskirts of the city. The slow death of hope that some members of her family might have survived made Mother even angrier than she had been during the war. After a time she stopped talking to others about them and would begin to cry if anyone asked about them.

I went to school for the first time and was caught up in the struggle to make a place in a world still sadly imbued with the attitudes that had generated so much suffering. All but a few of those who had opposed Nazism had been killed; all but a few of those who had supported Nazism returned to work. Frequently in trouble because I wouldn't let racial or ethnic slurs go unchallenged, I carried with me like a secret talisman the vision of Frau Pimber's full moon and often wished that I could flash it at teachers or fellow students who hadn't learned from our recent history.

Chapter 7

Liberation

The joy of having escaped death by the hands of war made the unearthly ruins of Hamburg seem to me more like a smoldering paradise than the purgatory other people thought our once lovely city had become. After years of fear and hiding I skipped down rubbled streets, ignoring an occasional whiff of decayed flesh, flashing a smile and a thumbs-up at every Tommy I saw. Remembering the bullets that answered my attempt to thank a newly arrived liberator, I never tried that again, even though it soon became clear that such a response wouldn't be repeated. Despite being self-conscious about my thumbs, which were noticeably shorter above the knuckle than those of other girls, I held them up defiantly because I desperately wanted the British to know that I wasn't like the rest, that Winston Churchill was my hero, that I was glad they had come and I wanted them to stay to protect the handful of Jews who had somehow survived.

The bombings had left me with such a fear of fire that my heart would begin to pound whenever I heard a siren, and something within me would shiver long after the sound died away. A helmeted fireman haunted my dreams, night after night climbing a tall ladder until the wall it was leaning against collapsed in a shower of sparks. He fell toward the flames in a graceful arc, but never quite reached them because I would awaken and conjure up pleasing mental images, such as poppies or fireflies. Having been trapped for hours beneath smoking rubble and later forced to hide in an earthen dugout, I was extremely uncomfortable in enclosed spaces and dreaded elevators, tunnels, cellars, and windowless rooms. I was also acutely aware that thousands of Hamburg's children had been killed or maimed by the bombings, possibly even more than had been condemned to death for being Jews. And I hated all such killing with a passion that I couldn't always control.

At the same time I was glad that the intensive bombing of Hamburg by the British and the Americans during the summer of 1943 had enabled my mother and me to escape being sent to a death camp. Even though the bombardiers of Operation Gomorrah obviously had not intended to save lives, they had derailed our deportation by destroying most of Hamburg and tens of thousands of its women and children. Since we had lived near the center of an all-consuming firestorm and we were not allowed to use the bomb shelters, the authorities who had ticketed us for Auschwitz assumed that we must have been among the thousands who were burned beyond recognition. And if the smile I flashed at British soldiers two years later sometimes appeared a trifle tightlipped, that was because I wanted other Hamburgers to see how I felt but was afraid of what they might do when the Tommies packed their gear, climbed back into their tanks and went rolling, rolling home.

Many Hamburgers must have felt some remorse for the incredible suffering Germany had inflicted, especially when they saw pictures of its extermination programs, such as the photo of a mountain of children's shoes at one of the death camps. That picture had made my father weep and place a large hand on my shoulder, while Mother had cried out and almost crushed my youngest sister in her arms. But most people seemed too embittered by their own war experiences to give much thought to the suffering of others, especially of people whom they had been taught to hate even before they had been taught their ABCs. Every Hamburg family had experienced losses, most of them in the ten days and nights of Operation Gomorrah, when some fifty thousand civilians had been killed. Long after those raids thousands of Hamburgers had to burrow beneath the rubble to sleep in cold cellars and basements. Whatever sparks of penitence smoldered beneath the ashes of the ruined city, the only expressions of regret I saw or heard in the streets and shops and schools of Hamburg were laments for the hardships of defeat.

Father pointed out to anyone who would listen that, bad as they were, conditions in Hamburg were not as harsh as those in many of the cities Germany had conquered, especially in Poland and Russia where starvation had been used as a weapon of extermination. But most Hamburgers were too miserable in the first years of occupation to concern themselves with such comparisons. Exceptionally cold winters combined with shortages of food and fuel extracted self-pitying moans from people who had silently witnessed mass deportations and had stoically accepted the destruction of their city by Allied bombers.

Even though it was obvious to everyone that the RAF had targeted Hamburg's residential neighborhoods, few people seemed to be angry with the occupying British soldiers about that. Ignoring the fact that almost all the Jews had been deported before the most destructive raids, some people continued to complain that the bombers had spared Jewish houses. But just about everybody thought that Hamburgers were lucky to be occupied by the British, who were viewed as fellow seafarers with compatible prejudices and a wry sense of humor. General Montgomery's order forbidding his troops to fraternize with the locals probably didn't offend very many Hamburgers, however, since most were too reserved themselves to socialize with strangers.

For their part, the victorious Tommies didn't appear to be at all troubled by civilian casualties, whether caused by the RAF or by the

Third Reich, so long as the victims were Germans. They were upset about crimes against captured British soldiers and other breaches of the so-called rules of warfare. The Allies prosecuted handfuls of prominent Nazis for such offenses, adding charges that grew out of the murder of some ten million people because of their ethnic or religious classification. If they added charges for murdering people because of their unorthodox sexual inclinations, I was not aware of that, although it was common knowledge that large numbers of people denounced as homosexuals had been imprisoned and murdered by the Reich.

The triumphant Allies may have considered the trials of selected Nazis at Nuremberg as symbolic purification rites, like swinging canisters of incense in a gothic cathedral after the celebration of an auto-da-fé. Whatever the victors thought, their "denazification" program was mostly scented smoke. For all of the crimes of the Nazis' twelve-year reign of terror, fewer than a thousand monsters were severely punished. The vast majority of those who had participated in the various campaigns of mass murder were troubled if at all only by their own conscience. With but few exceptions the cogs in the killing machinery—the judges, bureaucrats, prosecutors, informers, military, and police officials who had made genocide happen—could look forward to well-oiled retirements. Industrialists who had starved and killed thousands of slave laborers were not even asked to open their Swiss bank accounts to treat the wounds of those who had survived. The most abusive slaveholder was pardoned by the Americans two years after his conviction for crimes against humanity and was given tens of millions of dollars to refire his furnaces. In the heat of the cold war, he quickly became one of the five richest men on earth.

Since economic atrocities were seldom considered grounds for prosecution, bankers who had financed aggression and fattened themselves on confiscation, even trading gold from the teeth of the murdered, were encouraged to reopen for business. Lions of the learned professions, which had purged their ranks of Jews and had refused to treat, teach or represent them, resumed their practices as if nothing upsetting had happened. So did many musicians, actors, entertainers, filmmakers, writers, and artists who had scorned Jewish colleagues and the works of Jews. The Bayreuth opera orchestra, which had serenaded the SS with music from Wagner's *The Meistersinger* as local Jews were being rounded up for slaughter, was soon playing the same stirring music for the Allied elite. Clerics who had preached hatred and publicly mourned the death of Hitler promptly remounted their pulpits. Teachers in the public school I attended ridiculed claims of genocide and at the same time assured students that we were subhuman anyway.

While British soldiers frequently returned my thumbs-up, their leaders were not keen to help surviving Jews or other Germans who had suffered at the hands of the SS or Gestapo. The fact that two of Father's brothers had been killed for opposing the Nazis didn't entitle their families to so much as an extra bucket of coal from the conquerors. Property taken from Jews, even something as prominent as a downtown department store or a mansion overlooking Alster Lake, often remained with unrightful owners or was taken over by the British for their own use. Although the Nazis had kept meticulous records of their crimes, there was little hope that Mother would recover her parents' confiscated Shakespeare First Folio, which apparently made its way across the English Channel, or any of their other valuable texts and works of art. Mother was too stunned and full of grief over the loss of her family even to think about pursuing former possessions, and the occupation authorities weren't much interested. Their attitude was that they had done their bit by defeating the German armed forces, and they didn't much care whether you were thankful or resentful, only that you not make trouble. The pudding-faced second lieutenant who had scorned my father's offer to help resettle refugees appeared to reflect the prevailing attitude.

When Mother rushed off from time to time to rescue a survivor still in detention or to interview someone who might know something about one of her relatives, she often entered a country where being German and a Jew earned her a double portion of hatred. Disregarding all dangers, she would leave home aglow with hope and would return days later in deep despair, possibly with a refugee in tow but never with a family member. I hated to see her hopes dashed and feared a return of the expression I had seen on her face the day she had tried to kill herself. When she seemed to be almost overburdened by sorrow, however, she would lift both our spirits by conspicuously defying a public rule or convention, as by refusing to stand in one of the lines that shortages and Occupation controls made ubiquitous. Instead she would walk to the head of a line and announce in a very loud voice, "You have always said that I'm not good enough to stand in line with you. So I won't force you to stand with me now." After letting that sink in for a bit, she would quietly demand and usually get whatever she had come for and depart with head high, followed by hateful looks and hissed epithets.

Unfortunately for me, my admiration of her independent attitude was not fully reciprocated. She greatly preferred children to be compliant. It was not that she was severely disapproving or that I was even slightly disrespectful. She sometimes scolded me, but not nearly as often as she scolded Helga. Instead, she would appear unhappy or put upon if I did something she didn't like. This was very effective because I adored her and would get terribly upset if anyone or anything made her sad. Since I was always trying to please her, her most effective tactic was to withhold praise, ignoring or appearing indifferent to any drawing or design or whatever I brought to her in the hope of winning a smile. Often, simultaneous approval of something Rena had done would salt my disappointment. But even though Mother seemed to be growing more distant as we both grew older, she continued to be my brave and beautiful hero, the savior who had held my hand and led me safely through the flames as the world exploded around us.

While my parents were at work, building shelters for the multitude of homeless in the early postwar years, I dutifully looked after my two younger sisters. I also played with them at times, but I didn't have any real interest in the things they wanted to do. Uncannily well-coordinated, Helga almost always wanted us to do something that was physically challenging. With wide, sea-green eyes and platinum pigtails, she didn't look much like a tomboy, but her movements were swift and deft and her idea of fun was to hang by her legs from an upper branch of a tree nobody else could climb. Although she was as thin as wire, she could outfight kids twice my size. When she threw a rock it always hit the mark. Seemingly fearless, she frequently flirted with danger, and I was as awed as I was grateful to have her as my defender. As might be expected she had occasional mishaps, such as when she fell headfirst into a huge pot of tar being used for street repair. She suffered superficial burns and had to be shorn of every platinum lock but was off and running again within minutes. Taken to a surgeon's office months later for removal of a plum pit from her ear, she popped it out like a champagne cork when she saw what had been done to another child who had been similarly reckless.

Helga was not as fortunate when she fell down a long flight of stairs, up which she had been pushing a neighbor's baby carriage. The baby was unhurt but Helga suffered a severe concussion and had to be taken to a hospital, where she was strapped to her bed because moving about too much might cause serious complications. But, as I discovered during a visit, when no one was watching she slipped out of her straps faster than I could say Harry Houdini and literally climbed the wall to look out the window. To my lasting regret I let my hatred of informers keep me from telling anyone. Later, she began to have terrible seizures.

Rena looked like a living doll and was treated like one by adults. If for any reason she didn't get her way immediately, a few tears from her dark blue eyes would quickly wash away all opposition. When she wanted us to play with dolls, however, I could not be moved. I didn't mind designing clothes for her dolls; in fact I rather liked that. But I had bitter memories of playing dolls with my one-time friend and neighbor, Monika, who had later refused to let me into the air-raid shelter during the deadliest bombing there had ever been. Rather than playing dolls with Rena or doing impossible acrobatics with Helga, I spent as much time as I could drawing, painting, or reading.

During the war, I had made pictures to help me stay calm during air raids and endure other lengthy periods when we were more or less confined to our apartment. I had saved these and shown them to my approving Father when he came home on leave. In hiding, the scarcity of materials had forced me to improvise by using leaves and wildflowers to make colorful compositions first sketched out in the dirt. These, of course, hadn't lasted but the desire to make pictures had remained strong. Having cut my teeth on adult literature during the war, after reading and rereading all my children's books many times, I had no interest afterwards in the fairy tales or other stories my sisters wanted me to read to them. Instead I was fascinated by books such as Thomas Mann's *Magic Mountain*, in part because it was about people suffering from consumption, which mirrored my own lung problems, but also because of its mysteriously complicated love relationships. Engrossed in such a book, I could not be moved by begging, bribes or even blows to indulge my sisters. As a result they said I was cruel and unfeeling.

As might be expected Mother sided with my sisters. She also seemed intent on saddling me with a childhood that war and personal inclination had made redundant. One of her ploys was to dress the three of us in identical outfits. I felt diminished by this but dropped my protest after it became clear that Mother and my sisters were hurt by my objection. Although I lost that battle, it stiffened my resolve to be my own person. I was well aware that I was not yet an adult, but I had seen too many horrors to pretend to be a little girl. To my dismay many of the things I wanted to know more about, my mother couldn't bear to discuss.

My feelings about the world as I knew it ran much deeper than mere distrust. I had seen what adults could do to children and I was angry. And the more I understood the enormity of Germany's crimes and the world's response, the angrier I became. For all practical purposes Germany had won the war against its Jews. There were only a few of us left. Genocide had succeeded. And though the posters depicting us as subhuman had been removed from Hamburg's public walls, the attitudes remained.

Hinter den Feindmächten: der Jude

One of many Nazi propaganda posters, which were displayed all over Hamburg. This one claims, with its message "Behind the Enemy Powers, a Jew," that Jews were to be blamed for instigating the war. (Source: United States Holocaust Memorial Museum)

Chapter 8

Refuge on the River

Fortunately for my sisters and me, some wealthy Hamburg Jews who had fled to America before the war, provided a temporary refuge from the persistent fear and loathing in postwar Germany. The Warburg family had been successful international bankers until their firm was Aryanized in 1938, at which point several members had emigrated to America where they acquired U.S. citizenship. Returning to Hamburg as a colonel in the American army in 1945, Eric (formerly Erich) Warburg found that the family's huge estate on the Elbe River in the village of Blankenese, where he had grown up, was being used as a German Army Hospital and was in danger of being commandeered by the British for their own use. Asserting the family's ownership rights, he proposed that the homes on the estate be used to house Jews who were still in concentration camps. This was amenable to the occupying authorities and attendant refugee organizations, and the estate was soon serving as a shelter for Jewish orphans from the pestilential Bergen-Belsen camp.

The school on the grounds of the Warburg estate was housed in a gleaming white mansion with a columned curved veranda and floor-to-ceiling windows that provided a dramatic view of the Elbe River beyond a formal garden and a scattering of trees. I loved it at first

Rena (left), Helga (center), and me (right) at the Blankenese school for surviving Jewish children.

sight for being so unlike the public school that had been forced to open its doors to me as a penalty for being on the losing side of the war. I also loved living by the Elbe, which had been the escape route I had fantasized about while lying in bed with my mother as the bombs had exploded all around us. My sisters and I were probably the only students in the school who had not lost one or both parents. Many of the children were the sole survivors of their families, and many of the staff had suffered losses and were wonderfully understanding and caring. Although few of the students had experienced much if anything in the way of formal schooling before coming to Blankenese, we were eager learners, and the staff members were equally interested in imparting their knowledge as swiftly as we were able to absorb it. Some of the instructors were eminent scholars, but they were as patient with us as if we were their grandchildren.

Encouraged by my father and by Sonia, a resident instructor with a husky voice who eschewed makeup and wore pants like a man, I looked forward to studying Hebrew. Sonia was not especially devout and neither was I, but she had lived in Palestine and considered the creation of a homeland for the Jews to be a sacred mission. When she told us about the ingenious and often dangerous efforts being made to get around the British embargo on the emigration of Jews to the tiny desert protectorate, she thrilled us with the idea that one day we might also engage in our own courageous and idealistic battles. She also provided us with an example of how to conduct discreet romances.

All of the older female students had been warned that improper physical contact with a male could spoil our chances for future happiness, ruining what was left of our lives. So of course we were wildly interested in learning as much as possible about every particular and treated the warning as a license to nag Sonia for specific details about what sorts of conduct might lead us to ruin and what we could get by with if we were clever. Sonia was very sympathetic and never made fun of our interest or our ignorance, but she could be devilishly vague. Sometimes, in response to a question, she would curl an arm around my neck or waist and speak so softly and confidentially that I was sure I was learning love's more intimate secrets. But her disclosures were so full of abstract allusions and the slang terms used by Sabras— Jews born in Palestine—that afterwards I couldn't be certain what she had told me. Other times, such as when several girls beseeched her for details about French kissing, she would laugh heartily and insist that we must be pretending ignorance to bedevil her.

"Since you speak French," she said, addressing me on that occasion, "you should know that girls your age are only kissed on the cheeks, if at all."

It was true that Mother had taught me French while we were in hiding. Although we didn't have a book, she was fluent and was able to teach me enough for us to communicate basic information privately in the presence of Germans who didn't understand the language. But it was also true that as a German Jew I had not had the benefit of schoolyard tutoring on subjects such as French kissing, while Sonia, growing up in Palestine, must have learned about these things long before she had reached my age. My dilemma was that I needed much more information but didn't want to admit my ignorance.

I decided that the best way to learn about sex from Sonia was to observe her behavior toward Pavel, a science instructor who was physically very dissimilar to her. She was dark and compact; he was green-eyed, fair, and gangling, looking as Aryan as anyone else I knew in Hamburg. Despite the ban on romantic entanglement, it was common knowledge that Sonia wanted Pavel to go with her to Palestine when their school contracts expired and he was equally determined that they should emigrate to America, where he intended to study and practice medicine.

"I'm not going to spend my life hoeing desert scrabble," Pavel had been heard to say more than once.

"You won't be hoeing," Sonia would reply. "You'll be creating a homeland that will need both doctors and farmers." To this, he would respond that as a European he needed rivers and trees and winters.

Mother (right) stands with our favorite Blankenese teachers behind Helga (left), Rena, and me (with puppy).

Almost all the boys and some of the girls at the school thought Sonia should give up on Palestine and go with Pavel to New York City. Although I thought New York would be a much more exciting place to live, I sided with Sonia because I knew how strongly she felt about creating a Jewish homeland and because it was fascinating to watch her slowly bend Pavel to her will.

I wanted Sonia to be my Hebrew teacher, but the headmistress gave that assignment to Dr. Liebewitz, who had once taught Hebrew at a Yeshiva in Leipzig. A soft-spoken and frail looking man, Dr. Liebewitz had been blinded by the SS because he had continued to teach privately after being forbidden to do so. As much as I admired his courage, I could not look at his face and could barely endure being in the same room with him. His scarred sightless eyes reminded me of how Uncle Freddie had looked after the Gestapo had beaten him to death. As a result I dreaded my Hebrew lessons and would have given them up had Sonia not implored me to continue.

I could tell that my squeamishness was causing Dr. Liebewitz great distress and this made me terribly unhappy, but I couldn't suppress my feelings. Without meaning to I would lower my voice until it was barely audible and gradually back away from him until I was sitting or standing halfway across the room, angling toward the door. Since oral communication was the primary medium of instruction, my action made us raise our voices unnecessarily and contributed to the tension between us. Feeling guilty I would move back to within reasonable proximity, but the atmosphere would remain charged and my proclivity to inch away would begin again. When at last his patience was exhausted, he removed his dark suit jacket, put it on the back of his chair and told me quietly but firmly to come and stand beside him.

I wondered if he wanted to chastise me in some way, but he gently admonished me not to be afraid. Then he asked me to place my hands on his shoulders, which I did after hesitating only a moment, and he then placed his much larger hands on my upper arms. Then he began slowly to feel and squeeze my arms and shoulders slightly, tracing the line of my clavicles with his thumbs and then extending his arms further and moving them around my neck and over my shoulder blades. He then paused, and I began to examine him in the same manner, holding my breath at first but pressing hard enough on the fabric of his shirt to feel the bony ball and socket underneath. After some fumbling, I located and traced his long collarbones, then slid my fingertips inside his collar and around his neck, then out and over his shirt-back and suspender straps to press the stiff wing-like plates beneath. He then cupped my chin in his hand and proceeded swiftly but meticulously to examine every part of my face with his fingertips, noticing, I felt sure, that my right ear stuck out a tiny bit more than the left one. When he had finished, he gave my nose a little tweak and smiled.

I was not as thorough as he had been, but I had no difficulty touching him and I was not repelled by his faintly musty smell. The black and silver hairs that covered his jaws and chin felt like the shredded wheat that was shipped in little boxes from Battle Creek, Michigan, for our breakfast tables. I lingered a bit on his large ears, lightly passed over his nose and eyes, and finished by slightly dislodging the round cap of embroidered felt that nestled in slightly damp curls on the top of his head.

"Excuse me!" I said in Hebrew. His smile widened, revealing one or two shiny gold teeth.

"I can tell that you're an intelligent young girl," he said, readjusting his yarmulke, "and now that we have been formally introduced I hope that we will be good friends."

I looked at his eyes and tears formed in mine but I didn't feel the urge to retreat. Instead, I put my arms around his neck and kissed his cheek. In time I became fluent in Hebrew and he became my first male confidant. I wouldn't ask his advice directly but would tell him as dispassionately as possible about people or events that bothered me. He would relate this to something that had happened in his past or something he had read or heard about and then would ask what I thought about it. If he didn't agree with my analysis he would ask further questions, finishing with an observation or a quote from the Torah that told me he understood my position but thought it deserved further consideration. I was amazed to find that he didn't hate the Nazis and their collaborators half as much as I did.

He told me that even civilized people may behave badly if they believe they have been treated unjustly.

I once ventured the opinion that Jews might believe in justice but justice didn't believe in us.

"You're right that our beliefs may generate hostility," he replied, "but we must strive for justice even when this inflames our own people. This is our conviction, our faith."

Looking at Dr. Liebewitz and marveling at his resistance to the Nazis I felt ashamed that I had rudely questioned the basis for his belief, but this didn't stop me from challenging pieties by him or anyone else at the school. The notion that Jews were "the chosen" people really put me off and would have, I think, even if the murder of millions had not been so fresh. After so much unchecked slaughter, it was impossible for me to believe that the all-powerful God of Jews and Christians was anything but a myth.

Despite my religious qualms, I enjoyed my Hebrew lessons and became Dr. Liebewitz's star pupil. Except for math, I enjoyed my other studies as well and various extracurricular activities such as music, drawing, and dancing. And I greatly appreciated access to a small but well-stocked library. I even enjoyed one sport, soccer, and believed I was the best goalie in school. Like most of the children at the school I was outwardly calm during waking hours and able to laugh and play and conceal my rage. But there were some who were more easily upset than the rest of us and a few who experienced serious difficulty controlling their emotions. And then there was Uri.

* * *

Uri came to the school in the middle of a term, which was not unusual since the process of sorting out refugee children continued for years. What was exceptional was his refusal to communicate with anyone about anything, which naturally sparked gruesome speculation as to what he must have experienced. Although the adults wouldn't discuss this with us—they just said to "act natural" around him—a consensus developed among the students that Uri must have seen his parents murdered or been made to work as one of the camp commandos who removed the dead from gas chambers and carted them to the crematoriums. When I asked Sonia if either theory was correct, she confided that she didn't know any more than we did.

The first time I saw Uri—I didn't "meet" him since he refused to acknowledge my greetings or even look my way—I concluded that he probably hadn't told anyone his story. He was several years older than I was—I couldn't tell how many—and taller, with a crooked nose, high cheekbones and large eyes whose corners seemed to be pulled back toward his ears, showing a lot of white. His stiff, straight hair looked like it had never been combed or brushed, but he frequently ran his fingers through it. Although he stared intently at everyone and everything, he refused to respond to questions by as much as a nod. By force of will he created an invisible perimeter that others couldn't cross.

After Uri had been at Blankenese for a few weeks, I told him that I was being taught Hebrew by a man who had been blinded by the Nazis and that he wished Uri would visit him. Uri didn't respond the first two or three times I suggested this, but eventually he followed me to Dr. Liebewitz's study and allowed the professor to examine his head and torso with his fingertips. Even in the dim light I could see that Uri trembled as he was being examined. After that, however, he served silently as Dr. Liebewitz's helper and guide, and the professor became his tutor. Uri became calm and responsive when he was with the professor and the two must have talked when they were alone, since Dr. Liebewitz was able to relate some of Uri's background to me.

From the good doctor I learned that Uri was from a town in western Hungary, near the border with Austria. He and his parents and an older sister had been arrested by the Nazis and sent to Auschwitz, where his parents had been gassed and cremated, and he and his sister had been selected to work as slave laborers in one of the factories. After the Russian army had battled its way to the Polish border, Uri and his sister had been transferred from Auschwitz to a factory in the west. A few months later that plant had been bombed and many of the slave laborers had been killed, possibly including his sister, although Uri hadn't been very specific about how his sister had died.

Although he understood and could speak German, Uri refused to speak with anyone but the headmistress and Dr. Liebewitz for quite some time. He continued to take classes and would write some exercises, but he would become visibly upset, sometimes almost violent, if a teacher pressed him for more. He didn't attack people but would bang furniture, plumbing, dishes and other objects with his fist or whatever he had in his hand. When I asked Dr. Liebewitz how the rest of us should react to Uri's behavior, he counseled patience.

"Uri needs more time," he would say, "and he needs our friendship. We must be patient friends until he feels that he can trust us. Then he will be fine."

Perhaps because most other children seemed insufferably impressionable and most adults seemed somewhat artificial to me, I felt a special affinity for Uri. Although he was much more extreme, we both preferred to remain outcasts rather than become the sociable tools others wished us to be. Or so I told myself, since I very much wanted him to like me. There were times when I thought he might, at least a little, but if he did he still wouldn't allow me to get close or have any real exchange of views. The only person he seemed to trust was Dr. Liebewitz. So I tried to get closer to Uri through my tutor. The obvious way to please Dr. Liebewitz was to excel in my study of the language, so I concentrated on learning Hebrew with an ardor that surprised even me. To my teacher's delight and mine, I made astonishing progress very quickly. Since I knew that Uri was being taught Hebrew in a more indirect fashion by our tutor, I was eager to impart my quick grasp of the language to him. I imagined that he might be able to say the things in Hebrew that he couldn't bring himself to say in German.

But Uri and just about everyone else except Dr. Liebewitz seemed more put off than charmed by my accomplishment, as if I had breached some unwritten covenant by making a difficult subject seem easy. My mother was especially nonplussed because I accompanied my interest in the language with also embracing the practices of the Hebrew religion. Here again I was motivated primarily by a desire to get closer to Uri, who seemed to be responding positively to the religious instruction gently administered to him by Dr. Liebewitz. So I didn't let my lack of belief prevent me from being an ardent practitioner of the ritual. Because of the genocide, and now also because of my feelings for Uri, I wanted to identify with Judaism. I also thought my display of devotion would please my mother, because her mother had been deeply religious although she hadn't often gone to temple. Most of all I wanted to repair the troubling rift in my relationship with Mother. Although she was still my hero, a crack in our relationship had appeared soon after the war ended and seemed to widen further every year. But, instead of helping, my observance of dietary and other religious rules served to increase the distance between us. She was, I discovered, quite snootily secular.

The only person other than my tutor who was genuinely pleased by my headlong plunge into Judaism was my father. He had told me more than once that I had a duty to stand up and speak up for those who had been killed. And as a reward for my success in learning Hebrew, he gave me an expensive watch even though it was a very lean year for anyone not connected to the black market or the British occupation. Father knew that I had longed for a watch for some time and took me to a fine old shop in Blankenese so that I could pick it out. I chose a watch that looked suitable for either a boy or a girl. And I couldn't wait to get back to school to give it to Uri.

When I handed Uri the watch and told him it was his to keep so that he would always know the exact time, he looked it over very carefully and turned the winding knob a few times between his thumb and forefinger, testing the action. Then he hurled it as hard as he could against a stone wall. I may have gasped but I didn't move or say a word. I was stunned but I also wanted to appear calm. Without seeming to glance my way he walked over and examined the watch where it lay in the driveway. Apparently it was still running because he then stomped on it several times.

"I don't need a watch!" Uri said almost sadly. "It's always now!"

I wasn't completely sure what he meant or whether he was speaking to me or to himself. But I was thrilled by the possibility that he might open his feelings to me.

"Yes, of course," I said. "I don't need it. I just thought you might like it." I ransacked my brain for something to keep our first conversation going. "I have a book in Hebrew that you would probably like better," I said, "I can get it for you if you like."

Uri didn't respond or appear to take any notice of my offer, but instead headed toward his room, which he made clear was strictly off-limits to me. I walked over and picked up the watch, wondering what I would tell Father. The watch looked to me to be beyond repair. I didn't intend to find out. The one thing that seemed certain was that I couldn't tell Father or anyone else what Uri had done. There was no telling what might happen if I did. I decided that the best course would be to pretend to lose the watch and, if possible, to do that in such a way that the loss would be attributed to bad luck rather than carelessness. I realized that it needed to be done quickly before Helga or Rena found out and started asking a lot of questions I wouldn't want to answer. So I walked immediately to the front of the building and found a counselor who was wearing a watch and asked him the time, telling him that I needed to set my watch. I then ran to a spot where a clump of large stones bordered the Elbe River. Standing on a rock at the water's edge I pretended to wind the already defunct watch, then closed my eyes and fell into the river, flinging the watch as far as I could toward the deep. Although I was a good swimmer I yelled for help, which quickly arrived. Back on the bank, shivering and scraped, I lamented the loss of my new watch and was told to be glad that I hadn't drowned.

Father and everyone else seemed to accept my loss as an unfortunate accident. Everyone but Uri. I didn't attempt to talk with Uri in the days following the incident but neither did I try to avoid him. The sly truth was that I was more attracted than repelled by his rejection of an expensive watch. After I had given it to him, I told myself, it was his to do with as he wished and therefore no skin off my nose if he chose to destroy it. At the same time I didn't want to give the impression that I would be friendly no matter what he did to offend me. So I adopted an attitude of polite indifference to whatever he was doing. And it worked. About a week later, when no one else was around, he spoke to me again.

He said that I had behaved stupidly when I jumped into the river. He said this matter-of-factly and tried to maintain the same tone when I told him I had jumped because I didn't want my father to tear him limb from limb.

"He wouldn't," Uri said, letting a smile split his wide lips.

"No, he wouldn't, not over a watch. But I didn't want him to think I didn't appreciate his gift."

"Then, why did you give it to me?"

"Because I was stupid enough to think you would appreciate it."

"I did, but I didn't want it. In the camps, only the guards had watches."

"We're not in a camp."

"I know. Sometimes I forget."

Mother with Rena (left), me (center), and Helga (right) at Blankenese.

Chapter 9

Uri's Story

After our brief exchange about the watch, Uri began to talk to me whenever we were alone, and I began to contrive ways to make that happen. Otherwise I might have to wait days to hear the end of a story that had been broken off at its most interesting point because someone else had come within earshot. One of the first things I asked him was whether, as many at the school believed, he had stopped talking because he had seen his parents get killed.

Uri said that he hadn't seen that happen, that he had been separated from them before they were killed, but that he had later seen his dead mother being carted to the crematorium.

"What did you do?" I asked. He started to speak, but then some other children came near us, pretending to be interested in the flowers growing nearby but really trying to eavesdrop, and he hurriedly walked away. I trailed after him, but he refused to talk any more that day. When I finally found myself alone with him two days later, however, he took up where he had left off.

Uri said that when he saw his mother on the cart, he didn't recognize her at first. She was naked and they had cut off all her hair, but her eyes were open and staring at him. She seemed to be trying to say something but couldn't get the words out. He had started screaming and trying to pull her out from under the other bodies. But another prisoner had knocked him to the ground and covered his mouth to silence him.

"How horrible!" I said, regurgitating the memory of naked dead bodies in the streets of Hamburg. I asked him about the other prisoner.

Uri said that he had saved his life, that a guard would surely have killed him if he had kept screaming. Uri's voice was sad and I reached out to touch him. But he pulled back quickly and refused to say anything more, although he didn't walk away this time. Instead we both walked down to the river and sat on the rocks and watched the freighters and British warships plying the Elbe.

The next time we talked I tried to suggest that we had things in common. I told him that my grandmother, my uncle, and my aunt had been deported to a death camp at Minsk, which wasn't so far from Auschwitz. I also said that I would have been at Auschwitz with him if it hadn't been for the firebombing of Hamburg. We had already received a deportation order, I explained, but then the bombers came and killed so many people we were able to get away. The British and the Americans took turns, I said, the RAF at night and the Americans during the day. But I conceded that Auschwitz must have been even worse.

Uri said it had been very different. Prisoners had prayed for bombers, but nobody had been listening. He also said that I would have been killed my first day, since I would have been considered too young for work. He didn't explain how he had avoided the gas chambers but did say that he had been helped several times by other prisoners. One man, a teacher like Dr. Liebewitz only not as old, had taught him how to keep going when he was ready to drop.

"You do this," he explained, "by first making yourself tense all over, tightening every muscle as much as you can. Then you relax and let yourself sort of float. Do that three or four times," he said, "and you feel recharged with energy."

I said that it sounded simple, and he agreed that it was. He said he had recharged standing up and even during a march and that it had saved him several times. He added, however, that there had been times when nothing helped.

I asked what else he had learned, and he said that a man had taught him about weeds and mushrooms and other things he could eat. Other men had helped him in different ways. "A man who had sold women's underwear told wonderful stories that made people laugh, and there were other old men who told good stories," he recalled.

When Uri talked with me again a few days later, I asked him about his work at Auschwitz. He told me that at first he had been assigned to heavy manual labor, hauling rocks, sacks of cement, digging lines for pipes or latrines, or any other dirty job they wanted done. Then an old man who pushed a two-wheel cart bribed enough people to get Uri assigned as his helper.

"We hauled everything, including dead bodies," Uri said. The man could have made Uri do all the hard work, but he did his share for as long as he lasted.

Once Uri started talking with me, he also began to participate more fully in classroom activities. Yet he still wouldn't converse with anyone else except the headmistress and Dr. Liebewitz, and he wouldn't talk with me if others were present. So we began to walk along the river together or sit on the seawall or do whatever it took to find privacy. This caused considerable consternation for some of the faculty and other students who didn't think we should have special privileges or be allowed to avoid sports or meals or anything. There were even some who said that we were sneaking away to do naughty sexual things, a charge that literally took my breath away when I heard about it from Sonia. If they think I'm capable of doing that, I thought, maybe I am. I told Sonia more or less what was going on and why, leaving just enough of a hole in my story for a tiny seed of doubt. She told me to keep talking with Uri and not to worry about the others.

After dinner one evening in late August, while Sonia was reading to other students a mystery novel I had already read, Uri and I sat on the rocks beside the Elbe, facing each other so that we could see both the river and the mansion. After a little prodding, Uri talked some more about his experiences at Auschwitz. He told me that until they were too sick or weak to care, most of the slave laborers at the camp had tried to track the progress of the warring armies, each person praying for liberation or an armistice that would set him or her free. Although he had never stopped thinking and dreaming of release, Uri had given up on prayer. If praying could have helped, he said, the camp would have been empty.

He had also stopped paying attention to the rumors that passed for war news. Instead, he had focused his energy on "finding" things that he could trade for food or favors, such as being allowed to visit his sister, Judith, who worked in an arms factory in another part of the camp. The things he "found" he actually took off the dead people he had to remove from the barracks and cart to a crematorium while the living were at work. No one living or dead had much of anything but occasionally Uri had found something, such as an amulet or coin that could be used to bribe a guard. But nothing could have bought him a ticket out of Auschwitz, so he was as fearful as he was surprised when he was told in August 1944 to board a train that had just brought hundreds of prisoners into Auschwitz and was being refueled to take hundreds away.

* * *

Heading west toward the sunset Uri listened to several of his fellow prisoners debate where they were going and why. One of these boxcar lawyers pointed out that they weren't the first to leave Auschwitz at a time when new trainloads were still arriving from the far corners of Europe. Weeks earlier, when the Red Army had begun to approach Poland's western gates, the Krupp Company's automatic weapons plant and many of its workers had been transferred to a "safer" location in Silesia. Since no one knew the destination of the present train or why almost all its boxcars had been filled with women, every conceivable possibility was examined with care. The only point on which all agreed was that release from captivity was not a likelihood. Eventually a consensus developed that they were being transferred to new work sites within Germany, where, with enough slaves and hostages at its disposal, the Third Reich would be able to hold off the Allies indefinitely. In time England and America would agree to terms to keep the Red Army from taking Germany's industrial heartland and pitching its tents on the shores of the Atlantic.

Although everyone knew the Nazis were insane, no one in the boxcar believed that the German army would continue to fight on German soil until every last man and boy had been killed or captured. So several of the prisoners were lamenting that this new deportation might diminish their chances of being liberated. Others insisted it was better to be leaving Auschwitz since the Germans would never allow their slaves to be taken alive. Uri didn't pay much attention to the arguments. He thought that he had seen his sister, Judith, among the hundreds of women being loaded onto the train and nothing else mattered nearly as much as contriving to see her face-to-face at the first opportunity.

When the train finally arrived at a slave depot in the Ruhr area of Germany, however, Uri was too disoriented to attempt an immediate reunion with his sister. After several days in a cramped space with little food or water, every muscle and bone felt like it had been hit with a hammer, and he seemed to have lost the ability to tell whether he was awake or asleep. At first, the depot seemed to be a figment of one of his waking dreams. The smell of burning flesh emanating from Auschwitz crematoriums, which had remained in his nostrils throughout the long journey, was suddenly replaced by the astringent odor of burning coal. And instead of being wedged into a wooden bunk in fetid barracks infested with vermin, he was consigned to a cot in a large canvas tent that literally breathed the night air. Even

One of the Essen munitions factories of "Cannon King" Alfried Krupp. (Source:
The New York Times Current History of the European War*)*

the soup served up by the local slaves was infinitely superior to the bilge on which inmates had steadily declined at Auschwitz. But these improvements, as welcome as they were, did not fully account for the almost dream-like atmosphere of the slave depot.

The simultaneous unloading of several hundred Jewish women in their late teens or early twenties created that illusion. As they flexed sinewy arms and legs and turned stiffened backs and necks, their pale, shaved heads became incandescent in the slanting late-afternoon light and seemed almost to float above their gray prison frocks. Despite the sunlight and the baleful stares of guards with whips and truncheons, their eyes widened as they took in the huge pavilion tents in which they were to sleep. Watching one of them finger a tattooed number on her forearm, and another the pale yellow star on her sleeve, and seeing their faces cautiously accept the possibility that their lives had taken a dramatic turn for the better, Uri felt tears begin to trickle down his grimy cheeks.

When he and his sister were finally able to embrace a few days later, however, they were both too thrilled for tears. Judith had thought that he was still at Auschwitz and was overjoyed to find that they had both been transferred to the Ruhr depot, which seemed almost like summer camp by comparison. He was delighted to discover that, although she looked thin, the heavy physical work she had performed at Auschwitz had made her almost as strong as he was. When he commented on how wiry she was, Judith challenged him to arm wrestle, which enabled them to laugh together for the first time since they had been deported from Hungary. When she suggested that they pray together for their parents and sisters, he didn't object, but he couldn't make his lips repeat the words with her.

About ten days later Uri and the other men who had been on the train were ushered into a large open-sided tent for inspection by slave selectors, whom a depot official identified as representatives of the Reich's foremost armaments manufacturer, Alfried Krupp. Almost two weeks of pleasant weather and light duties in a camp with hundreds of young women, including one named Erika who initiated him into the transcendent pleasure of sex, had caused Uri to relax his defenses somewhat. So he was not mentally prepared when he suddenly confronted a gray-bearded man with a clipboard, a large fountain pen, and the skeptical look of a horse trader eyeing a Gypsy pony. As the slave selector pursed his lips and peered at him through small, silver-rimmed glasses, Uri realized that he was the youngest person anywhere around and that the selector might therefore consign him to the nearest extermination camp. To indicate that he was fit for hard work, Uri began to run in place and pummel his skinny torso with his fists. The selector stepped back with a disapproving sneer. A half-second later a guard struck Uri across his back and shoulder with a leather-covered truncheon.

Uri fell to his hands and knees and fought to hold back tears. Very quickly he stood up again, hoping to demonstrate that he was strong enough to take such a blow and keep going. Apparently this worked; the selector smiled slightly as he examined Uri's meager muscles. Muttering his misgivings, the selector pointed with a gloved finger to a group of men forming deeper within the tent.

Seeing that the group included the more able-bodied of the men who had been in his boxcar, Uri shuddered with relief then reached back reflexively to touch the area between neck and shoulder where the truncheon had landed. Feeling a stab of pain, Uri cried out and then scurried toward the group of men. But the Krupp selector shouted for him to halt and Uri instantly froze.

"We must teach this young man German discipline," the selector declared. "See to it that he goes to Dechenschule!"

The guard, who was wearing a blue uniform instead of the usual brown, gray, or black, promised to take care of it personally. He didn't hit Uri again but pushed and poked him with the square-sided truncheon to a position nearer the center of the tent. Told not to move a muscle until the guard returned for him, Uri waited and watched as the Krupp officials processed the remaining few men with brisk efficiency, accepting all but two or three. The gray-bearded selector pointed his pen at the rejected men and shouted to an SS official, "Send them to Buchenwald and bring in the Jewesses!"

Minutes later scores of frightened young women in prison garb were herded into the tent. They stumbled about frantically in their galoshes and dilapidated shoes, repeatedly bumping into one another and sometimes screaming as a leather bullwhip split their flesh with a lightning crack. The wielder of the whip, a stout SS captain with a truncheon in his other hand, sauntered behind them, scowling and somehow smiling at the same time. Although his legs were short and his shoulders broad, the captain skipped about with a dancer's agility until his shiny black boots deftly positioned him to strike whatever precise point on a woman's anatomy his reptilian mind had selected. Male and female SS guards helped him corral the women in front of the Krupp selectors, who acted as if they were watching an animal tamer in a circus tent. "Ja! Ja!" they shouted in unison each time he struck a woman with his whip, and they broke into spontaneous applause when he knocked one woman's eye from its socket and onto the tarmac. As the stricken woman and those close to her fell to their knees and screamed, a young woman quickly retrieved the bloody eye, receiving as punishment a painful lash that struck the Red Cross on the back of her prison frock.

Recognizing the retriever of the eye as the girl who had relieved him of his virginity, Uri felt as if he had been castrated right where he stood. His legs trembled and the hot pain in his neck shot through his lower body. Although months of handling and disposing of the dead and dying had hardened his responses to suffering, the adroit cruelty of the SS captain and his applauding colleagues was more than Uri could stand. Tears coursed down his cheeks as he fought for control by telling himself that his sister was not among this group of women and by suppressing the thought that she might well be in the next. Fortunately the German work ethic soon overtook Baron Krupp's representatives, who temporarily sidelined the SS captain so that they could get about the business of selecting the fittest of the young women for their master.

The inspection of the women was much more thorough than the cursory examination given the men. The selectors complained loudly about the condition of the women but appeared to enjoy thumping the Red Cross on the back of every dress, lifting the skirts of many, and looking under the yellow star on each left sleeve to check for vaccination. Uri observed that every bulging tummy or swelling breast received special attention, and that the selectors seemed to be rejecting any woman who looked as if she might be pregnant. Such women were made to join a larger group at which the selector pointed and shouted, "Buchenwald!" Uri was convinced that these women were being condemned, so when Judith took her place on the slave block, Uri held his breath until his sister was thankfully consigned to the smaller group.

Long before the selection of female slaves was completed all of the other men who had been selected, but not Uri, were loaded onto trucks and dispatched to one of the fifty or more slave compounds in and around the city of Essen. Groups of thirty or forty of the selected women were allowed to return to their sleep tents for personal belongings and then were also loaded onto trucks. As she left the selection tent Judith surreptitiously waved to Uri. He wanted to respond but didn't dare because she was passing within the range of the SS officer with the long whip. After she had moved beyond the reach of the lash Uri waved back, but he didn't think Judith had seen him. His back hurt and he felt utterly alone.

A half hour later, when the captain started toward the entrance to the tent, Uri was somewhat cheered by the thought that he and Judith might never see that fiend again. On his way out, however, the captain was stopped by the slave selector who had chosen Uri. Uri couldn't hear what was said, but as the selector spoke, the captain's eyes methodically searched the shed until they found Uri. The captain smiled with tight lips and the corners of his mouth turned down, then he touched the leather visor of his hat with his whip and marched out of the tent.

Accompanied by the blue uniformed guard who had struck him with the truncheon, Uri climbed into the rear of the last truck leaving the depot. They joined a group of agitated young women who didn't know where they were being sent. Some feared that they were the ones who had been selected for extermination while others lamented that the friends left behind would soon be murdered. Listening to their conversations in Czech and Hungarian and Romanian, Uri concluded that even those who were confident that they had been chosen as slaves were unaware that their new master was the head of Europe's most powerful and fabled family. Thinking they would want to know, Uri pointed to the name on the guard's hat. Although the guard had seemed absorbed in loading and lighting his steeply curved pipe, he noticed Uri's gesture and was aware that several of the women had curtailed their conversations and were looking at him. After a few quick puffs that made the pipe bowl glow like a miniature volcano, the guard exhaled a cloud of smoke and then pointed with the stem of his pipe to the name emblazoned in block capital letters on his hat, on his sleeve, and above the breast pocket of his shirt. The dark eyes of the young women shifted as he proudly made his point, "KRUPP. KRUPP. KRUPP."

He took another puff and pointed the pipe stem toward the countryside beyond the truck. "Krupp is master here," he said, rotating the stem to take in the entire landscape. He warned them to work very hard to keep from being sent to Buchenwald.

Like most Europeans the women were aware that the Krupps were the famous "cannon kings" whose weapons had killed more people than the plagues. They associated the name with those of monarchs and earlier, more chivalrous wars, as well as with Hitler and the Third Reich's triumphs. After a respectful pause, the women returned to their conversations in Romanian, Czech, and Hungarian as the truck rolled through a landscape cluttered with factories, refineries, power plants, forges, mines, smelters, laboratories, foundries, rolling mills, cement plants, firing ranges, kilns, air strips, and launch pads.

"Big Bertha," one of the women said suddenly, referring to the Krupp matriarch after whom the firm's most famous cannon was named, "I'll bet she lives around here somewhere."

The guard nodded his head and relit his pipe.

The expressions on the women's faces grew even brighter as the truck bullied its way through the bustling streets of Essen, where trolleys, trucks, motorcycles, bicycles and pedestrians noisily competed for the right of way. The presence of so many people suggested to Uri and all the women that conditions might not be so bad with so many witnesses about. The guard, however, continued to look glum and hardened his demeanor even more when the truck braked to a halt on Humbolt Strasse at the entrance to Alfried Krupp's concentration camp for Jewish women. Uri could see through curtains of barbed wire that other women who had been at the depot had preceded them. They were standing in military formation in front of the dormitories, which looked more or less like the ones at Auschwitz. Each woman had a thin blanket folded over her left arm. Mindful of the armed guards in the watchtower that loomed above him, Uri tried without success to spot his sister among the large group of women.

Immediately after the women on Uri's truck entered the camp they were issued blankets and wooden clogs and made to line up with the others. Martial music suddenly blared from loudspeakers attached to the guard towers and after only three or four minutes stopped just as abruptly. In the silence that followed Uri could hear the braking and clanging of trolleys at a station adjacent to the camp. Then he noticed the black uniformed figure striding toward the women from a smaller building across the field from the dormitories.

"No! No! No!" Uri groaned to himself as the stocky SS officer who had terrorized the women at the slave depot came to a halt in front of them and began to bark out instructions. The guard who had ridden on the truck with Uri tapped him on his sore shoulder and pointed toward the SS officer, who was underscoring his harangue by cracking his whip.

"The Camp Commander," the guard said, eliciting more muffled groans from Uri. The guard then turned Uri around and shoved him until he began to walk on his own down the street leading away from the camp. Then the guard got on a bicycle he had obtained from a small round shed near the trolley station and pedaled beside Uri, compelling him to run at a dogtrot. Uri was too upset to care that his ill-fitting Auschwitz shoes were rubbing huge blisters on his feet. All he could think about was how his sister and the other women must have felt to find themselves at the mercy of the fiend they thought they had left behind at the depot.

Dechenschule concentration camp was less than two miles from the Jewish women's camp but seemed a lot longer to Uri because, for one thing, his feet were painfully raw and, for another, he hated every step that separated him from his sister. His feet would have been even worse if he hadn't taken off his shoes and run barefoot over the smooth cobblestones that paved Essen's streets. The two barracks at Dechenschule were made of stone and looked like school buildings, which is what they had been before the windows were fitted with iron bars, the classrooms were crammed with three-tiered bunks, and the whole compound was wrapped in barbed wire. After he was registered and given a new number—his Krupp number—Uri was issued a blanket and an ill-fitting prison uniform whose stripes were yellow and robin's-egg blue. Both the blanket and the uniform were embossed with the overlapping three rings representing cannon muzzles that formed the emblem or logo of Krupp enterprises. He was instructed that the Krupp firm had converted Dechenschule from a school into a penal camp for slaves they wanted to isolate and punish. As punishment, inmates were compelled to perform the most difficult and dangerous tasks in Krupp's vast complex of mining, smelting, and manufacturing enterprises in and around Essen. The camp was under the auspices of the Gestapo but was staffed by SS-trained Krupp guards who, he was told, would shoot to kill anyone who made any move to escape.

Within a few days Uri learned that there were only a few real criminals or offenders at Dechenschule. Most of the inmates were there because they had been community leaders—public officials, doctors, teachers, judges, lawyers and even clergymen—who had been taken hostage in occupied countries to keep the populace in line. Once in custody they became subject to a Nazi regulation that mandated the deportation of anyone held for more than eight days without being charged or cleared. The Nazis carried out the deportations with utmost secrecy—they called the program "Night and Fog," thereby heightening the impact on families and communities by making leading citizens disappear without a trace.

Waiting to profit from their disappearance was the current cannon king, Alfried Krupp, the Third Reich's avid exploiter of slave labor. As the Third Reich's Fuehrer over all industry and the sole proprietor of its largest industrial complex, he demanded and obtained more than a hundred thousand slaves to help him produce the arms that enabled Germany to wage global war. Although he had slave colonies at many plants scattered about occupied Europe, most of his slaves were held in concentration camps in and around Essen. The Night-and-Fog victims in Uri's barracks came mainly from France, Belgium or Holland. Some thought that Krupp had placed them in his penalty compound because he feared they would be more motivated than others to escape. Others said he was simply going along with the policy of intensifying the pain of the prisoners and their families by enforcing secrecy. A French priest who supported Hitler as a bulwark against communism said their incarceration was a mistake that would surely be corrected by Baron Krupp when he became aware of it. He remained convinced even when told by another imprisoned priest, who cleaned Krupp's office every morning, that the slave chief was fully aware of the means by which his slaves were acquired. But whatever Krupp's reasons for treating them so vilely, most of his Night-and-Fog slaves resented being kept incommunicado as much as they hated the harsh conditions and back-breaking labor. Having become accustomed to hard labor at Auschwitz, Uri was not as disturbed by his treatment at Dechenschule as he was by his sister's nightmare ordeal on Humbolt Street.

Among Krupp's Essen slave colonies, Uri learned over time, the most wretched conditions appeared to be reserved for the Jewish women. He was unaware that Krupp had given his personal attention to the procurement and exploitation of this group, regarding it as something of an experiment to test whether women slaves could be used for heavy work that normally was assigned only to men. But like everyone else, Uri understood that Jews were considered the lowest form of slave life, to be treated worse than non-Jews from Eastern Europe, who were more abused than those from the West. With much greater anguish than others, Uri heard about or even witnessed the special mistreatment given his sister and her companions.

When the weather in northern Germany turned bitterly cold, all of the men and women in Krupp's fifty or so concentration camps in the area, including Uri's penal camp, had or were issued a second blanket, as SS rules required. All except the five hundred Jewish women on Humbolt Strasse; they were forced to get by with only one. Frequently they were forced to work with hot coals or metals that burned, cut, or froze their hands, but no protective clothing or gloves were permitted. Their only garment was the thin burlap prison dress they had been issued at Auschwitz, their shoes the crude open wooden clogs issued by Krupp. Although their work was as heavy and dangerous as any imposed on men, their rations, a bowl of soup and a slice of bread a day, were the skimpiest in Essen and the most frequently withheld.

Lack of protection from air raids needlessly killed thousands of Krupp slaves and everyone had priority over the Jewish women to any refuge that was available. When a raid occurred while they were at work, they were the only ones expressly forbidden to seek some kind of shelter. Jewish girls who in one instance took refuge in a partially destroyed cellar inside their camp's barbed wire were forced to yield this space to Polish men from another camp. In contrast to his sister, Uri could bury himself in a slag heap if he was working near one when an alarm sounded or could crouch in a ravine Dechenschule prisoners had dug at their camp to gain a measure of protection from bomb splinters. This was not enough protection to prevent scores of deaths at Dechenschule during one raid, but the Jewish women, whose barracks were destroyed in the same raid, had been forbidden to dig or lie in slit trenches, the narrow shallow trenches or ditches that others were allowed to use for a modicum of protection during raids. Women locked in one of the huts that was set on fire during that raid were burned alive because no guard would release them. After that raid the survivors at Dechenschule, including Uri, were transferred to another camp, but his sister and her companions were made to live partly exposed to the elements in the cold, wet and darkened ruins of the camp's kitchen.

During that last terrible winter of the war, after their wooden clogs had broken apart and their feet were bloody and oozing pus, the battered, starved, severely frostbitten women were marched barefoot for nine miles twice a day through the main streets of Essen, letting everyone see how the cannon king and his country dealt with Jewish women. To heighten their humiliation, the guards shaved grotesque patterns on the women's heads, the most derisive design being a Christian Cross to mock the Jew's "heathen" status. Alone among Krupp's hundred thousand slaves, the Jewish women were not allowed to use the toilets in the plants or foundries where they worked but were forced to go out in the open. From time to time the screams of one or more women being punished or tortured near Krupp headquarters reached the ears of the firm's top executives and directors. The response, if any, was simply to have a secretary close the windows.

When the Jewish women returned to their barracks at day's end, they were confronted by SS guards recruited by Krupp who beat them with metal truncheons at the slightest provocation or simply for sport. As the Allied armies drew closer, brutality grew more frequent and the guards taunted the women, saying that there would always be time to kill them before they could be liberated. But the most terrifying event of every evening was the arrival in the women's quarters of the short-legged SS Camp Commander. As every Krupp official and most of Essen knew, his specialty was putting out eyes with his whip. He also delighted in lashing other parts of the body and sometimes flayed women to death.

Accounts of such horrors circulated by word of mouth throughout the cannon king's domain, being told and retold countless times by both slaves and masters and driving Uri wild with fear for his sister. Lying on his wooden bunk at night, it was impossible for him to put images of the sadistic SS captain out of his mind whether he was awake or asleep. When he tried to replace such images with those of Erika, the spirited girl who had been his first lover, he compounded his suffering.

Despite their own dire condition, the members of Uri's working group from the disciplinary camp were moved to anger and pity by the brutalized state of the Jewish women who marched past them at an Essen intersection as both groups were on their way to work. Frequently when he saw his sister among the marching women, Uri wanted to dash across the street, pull her out of the ranks, and attempt to escape with her. But he knew that he would surely fail and she as well as he would be severely punished or probably killed. One day as Judith passed from sight unaware that he was nearby, Uri resolved to do whatever it took to see her.

Drawing on his Auschwitz experience, Uri volunteered that same day to help recover and remove the bodies of those who had died in Krupp's service. In addition to those killed in air raids, which sometimes numbered several hundred, disease, malnutrition and other mistreatment were taking an increasingly heavy daily toll on the slave population. Tuberculosis and other contagious diseases were so prevalent that no one wanted to touch the dead. Because of this Uri got his wish.

With the help of bribes to civilian security personnel, Uri was soon able to arrange to see his sister at her worksite. She was so tired and emaciated that she seemed to look through him for a full minute before she recognized him. Her skin, which had remained supple and relatively smooth at Auschwitz, now looked like stiff butcher paper that had been reused several times. It was wrinkled, stained, torn, and spotted with dried blood and bites that might have come from rats as well as insects. Despite her appearance, however, Judith still had a strong will to live. Brother and sister quickly agreed that they should attempt to escape rather than wait to be freed, since they both believed that the guards meant it when they said they would kill all the Jewish women before the Allies arrived.

"The best time to escape," Judith said, "would be during a heavy raid, when the guards retired to their bunkers." Uri agreed and told her that when the next big raid occurred he would come to her compound and slip through a damaged part of the barbed wire that surrounded her camp. Uri had spotted the damage when his burial detail had gone to the cemetery that bordered the camp to dig a grave. He assured Judith that he would be able to get out of the camp to which he had been transferred after Dechenschule had been bombed. He also said he would try to identify a place to hide in Essen. Judith confided that she could probably get them a place by appealing to one of the older Krupp workers who occasionally slipped her a bit of food in return for being allowed to fondle her.

Judith soon persuaded one of her molesters to secure a place for her to hide. Uri confirmed that the damaged barbed wire at her camp had not been repaired and located a place where he could get through the wire at his camp using a metal stake that was meant to hold it down. He also got his hands on the coveralls of a Krupp employee who had died in a raid. But when Allied bombers failed to return to Essen for several weeks, Judith and Uri had to put their plans on hold.

During that time Uri's work took him to just about all the facilities for treating sick and injured Krupp slaves. He discovered that there were in fact few facilities, no medicine and very little treatment unless, as at Uri's own barracks, a slave with some medical competence was allowed to minister to the other inmates. That had been permitted because his camp's dispensary and sick bay, which were much too small for the numbers of ill inmates, were so stinking and filthy with human excrement that no Krupp employee wanted to go near them. In Krupp's Essen camps hundreds of injured and seriously ill slaves died every week without any medicine or antiseptics to discourage wounds from festering and becoming gangrenous. There was even a Krupp concentration camp for the hundreds of children who against all odds were born to slaves. The mothers were forced to return to work before the babies were weaned and many of the infants soon died. Identified only by their slave numbers, scores were buried in Essen by Uri's crew.

Overwhelmed by the enormity of their workload and the inhumanity that caused it, Uri asked a veteran gravedigger, a tall, skeletal, slightly stooped man with a French accent, if conditions for slaves had been better when the Germans were winning the war. They were digging a grave in a field that was partially covered with snow and Uri was shivering with cold even though he was wearing a dead man's sweater beneath his blue-and-yellow-striped prison garb. The veteran first glanced at the guard, an old Krupp hand who was making a small fire for himself from brush they had cut, and then put a finger to the side of his long nose.

He told Uri that the Krupps were in charge of all German industry and could always get anything they wanted, but that even when Germany ruled almost all of Europe and was stripping it of food, Krupp slaves were as underfed then as now. In good times as well as bad, conditions had always been harsh for Krupp slaves. When another digger suggested that Krupp might "fatten us up" a bit before the Allies arrived, the veteran said there was not a chance. "Germans still believe that Krupp and Hitler will come up with something to defeat their enemies," he explained, "and Krupp won't put doubts into cabbage heads by suddenly treating slaves like human beings."

A few days later Uri's anxiety for his sister's welfare spiked sharply when word spread in the camps that Krupp was arranging to ship the Jewish women to Buchenwald where they would be fed to the ovens to keep the Allies from seeing what he had done to them. Although the railways had been severely damaged by bombing, the veteran gravedigger warned that almighty Alfried could arrange to have the women disposed of by one means or another. He said that Krupp had always been Hitler's indispensable man. Without the Krupps Hitler would have been a comic opera figure. The Krupps had helped to make him Chancellor, but Alfried's mother wouldn't let Hitler, an "upstart corporal" spend the night in their castle when he came to thank them.

"How come you know so much about this?" Uri asked, drawn to this Frenchman who talked to him more than anyone else did.

The Frenchman said that he had been one of the lawyers for the owner of a tractor factory that Alfried Krupp had decided to take for himself. After learning everything he could about Krupp, the Frenchman had advised his client to sign over the factory. But the rightful owner refused. He came from such a powerful family himself that he thought he could say no to Krupp. This was a fatal miscalculation.

Uri asked if Krupp had caused the man to be arrested.

The Frenchman nodded his head. He said that his client was a Jew and had been sent to Auschwitz where he was promptly killed. At that point the Frenchman also had been arrested and had been made to "disappear" in Essen. Asked why his client had thought he could stand up to Krupp, the French lawyer explained, "He was a Rothschild, a member of the famous Jewish banking family headed by Baron de Rothschild."

After Krupp arranged for a special train to dispatch into oblivion all of the nameless inmates in his camp for children born to Krupp slaves, Uri bribed a guard to let him see his sister again. Outside the mill where Judith worked, he passed a woman who was bent over with her hands on her knees urinating on the ground. She looked almost more animal than human. The top of her head was bald but matted tufts of hair rose above her ears. Her tattered burlap dress was streaked and plastered to her body and her exposed legs and cheeks showed bloody welts. Shuddering at the thought that his sister might be in similar shape, Uri looked away and hurriedly shouldered through the heavy doors of the mill.

When he saw Judith there, he told her that Krupp had disposed of the slave children to keep the Allies from discovering them. He said that she should get ready to leave, since guards and prisoners were predicting that Krupp would soon send the Jewish women to the Buchenwald death camp for the same reason. Judith told him that she was aware of the situation but that they would have to wait for an air raid which would make the guards take to the shelters, since escaping together would be impossible while the guards remained at their posts. She drew a smile on his worried face by telling him she had secured a hiding place for them in Essen.

Before leaving her, Uri reassured Judith he would be able to get away when the planes came. He also asked her if it would be possible for them to take Erika with them. Judith told him that Erika had been given a terrible lashing by the Camp Commander and was in no condition to attempt an escape. Judith also expressed surprise that Uri hadn't seen Erika outside, since she had gone out to do her business just before he arrived. Realizing that the wretched woman he had passed outside was Erika, and that she had suffered so much he didn't recognize her, Uri pressed his hands over his eyes to hold back tears.

That night Uri's contraband coveralls were discovered inside his straw mattress by a guard who obviously had been tipped off about them. Although he insisted that he had taken the coveralls only for their warmth, Uri was accused of plotting an escape and the camp beater was immediately summoned. There had been no official beater at Dechenschule, and the survivors of the air raid that destroyed that camp experienced collective shock when they discovered to their horror that Neerfeld, the camp to which they had been transferred, employed a specialist to inflict pain.

The fearsome beater, a middle-aged man with dark hair and skin that looked like he had spent years shoveling coal into a Krupp furnace, was accompanied by a lanky SS lieutenant. The lieutenant's jackboots thundered on the floorboards as he walked through the barracks wrinkling his nose at the foul smell and demanding to see the prisoners who had tried to escape. Beneath his leather-billed hat, his pink face went scarlet when a Krupp guard pointed to Uri as the lone offender.

"A Jew boy!" the lieutenant bellowed, slapping his heavy leather overcoat with a swagger stick. He railed at the Krupp guards for interrupting his dinner for a Jew, telling them that the only way to deal with Jews was to shoot them. He asked for one of the guards to give him a gun since he hadn't brought his.

"First we need to find out who put him up to this," the beater advised, holding up Uri's coveralls with one hand while squeezing the back of Uri's neck with the other. He said that once Uri revealed who was plotting to escape with him, they could shoot the lot of them.

The lieutenant agreed. He called for a length of rope and removed his hat and overcoat, promising to discover Uri's confederates in short order. After the rope arrived, he quickly made a loop at one end and slipped it over Uri's head. He then threw the other end over a ceiling beam and jerked it sharply several times, tightening the noose until Uri was forced to stand on tiptoes, choking and gasping for breath. Whenever Uri grabbed at the noose to try to let in more air, the lieutenant would pull harder, almost lifting Uri off the ground, turning his face purple and causing his eyes to bulge and run with tears.

The beater meanwhile removed his own heavy coat and made one of the assembled prisoners pull Uri's blue-and-yellow-striped trousers down around his ankles.

"Oh this is a real Jew, alright," the lieutenant exclaimed, glancing at Uri's genitalia. He nodded at the beater who struck the back of Uri's pale thighs with his truncheon.

"Stop sniveling, Jewboy!" the lieutenant yelled. Easing up on the rope he ordered Uri to point out the men who were going to attempt an escape.

When Uri refused to oblige him, the lieutenant jerked on the rope and nodded at the beater, who struck with his truncheon again and again. After several blows Uri flailed the air with his arms as if to implicate everyone in the room, and the guards had to restrain the other prisoners from attacking him. Streaming mucus and tears, Uri released the contents of his bladder onto the floor. The lieutenant jerked hard on the rope as if to shut off the flow of water by cutting off the flow of air into Uri's lungs. Held aloft, Uri danced on air until he passed out. The lieutenant dropped him on the wet floor and told the beater to revive him. The beater tried for several minutes but was not successful.

"Don't ever disturb my dinner again for a Jew!" the lieutenant shouted, putting on his hat and coat. "Just shoot the bastard, because that's what I will do as soon as I see him." After he departed, the guards threatened to beat other prisoners until someone admitted that he was Uri's accomplice. A few men were clubbed but no one confessed. Soon the official beater left, quickly followed by guards. At the door, the senior guard shouted at the prisoners, "Clean up that filth!"

When the British Lancasters and Halifaxes returned to Essen several nights later, Uri was not sufficiently recovered from the beating to join his sister. He tried on deeply bruised legs, but they carried him no farther than the fence, where he became tangled up in Krupp-made barbed wire and collapsed. Judith, who had heard about the beating through the Krupp grapevine, started to leave her compound with a small group of women who were making their escape during the bombing raid, as she and Uri had planned. But after she had made her way through her camp's wire, she decided to return, thinking that if Uri somehow managed to reach her barracks, he would be captured and killed if she was not there to help him.

Before Allied tanks and other vehicles completely encircled the region, Krupp arranged for all the surviving Jewish women, including Judith, to be put on a special train to Buchenwald, where they and hundreds of other prisoners were to be killed. Not long after, the camp beater, the SS cadre and many of the guards disappeared. Although Uri was still unable to speak normally, because the rope had injured his windpipe, he had little difficulty obtaining clothes and escaping into the chaos of general collapse. To help him reach Buchenwald, the Frenchman gave Uri some money and a forged letter of safe transit signed with the name of a high Krupp official. He also told Uri where he had lived in France and invited him to visit after the war and to bring his sister. Uri nodded and pumped the hand of his skeletal friend in thanks.

By the time Uri reached Buchenwald, the American Army had liberated it. Unable to find his sister or any of the five hundred Jewish women dispatched from Essen, he finally pieced together enough information to figure out what had probably happened to them. He learned that in the last weeks of the war so many slaves had been sent to Buchenwald to be murdered that the killers

A photo taken during the liberation of Bergen-Belsen, where Uri searched for his sister.

there were overwhelmed. So they had rerouted several trainloads to other camps where it was thought there would be a better chance of killing the slaves before the Allies arrived. Since Bergen-Belsen was still in German hands and some of the trains had been sent there, Uri set out for that camp on a bicycle that had belonged to a Buchenwald guard.

After only an hour or so, however, Uri began to vomit the rich food the Americans had given him. He tried to continue but each time he ate something the vomiting recurred. As a result British troops reached Bergen-Belsen before he did. But what he saw there made him sick all over again. There were thousands of dead bodies in various stages of decay strewn over acres of bare ground within the huge compound. The Tommies had bulldozed mass graves that resembled huge swimming pools and were compelling the former guards to gather up the corpses one at a time and carry them, their dead limbs flopping about grotesquely, to the edge of the pit, where they would throw them one on top of another. Although he had great difficulty speaking, Uri was able to establish fairly quickly that Krupp's five hundred Jewish women had been brought to Bergen-Belsen and that some had been killed but many were still alive. No one whom he encountered could tell him what had happened to Judith, although several thought they might have seen her in the compound. They advised him to look for her in the facilities that had been established by the British for the hundreds who were gravely ill. Uri looked in all of the tents except those of people suffering from typhus or diphtheria, but didn't find her. Judith's name was not on any of their sick lists and the British would not allow Uri into the quarantine tents. He did, however, note that a patient in one of the typhus tents was named Erika.

Before dawn, while almost everyone in the area was asleep, Uri entered that tent and discovered the Erika he knew. Her head had been freshly shaven but her face still showed the marks of the lashing she had been given in Krupp's slave compound. He awakened her and she recognized him. Erika told him that Judith had been terribly worried about him after hearing about his beating and even more so after he was unable to come to her during the bombing raid. Judith had told her that he wanted to take her with them when they tried to escape.

"I couldn't have gone with you," Erika said, "but it made me happy to know that you wanted me to." Erika also told him that Judith had left their compound with two or three other women and had made it through the wire, but had come back in the hope that Uri would join her. She said that Judith had looked after her when the remaining women were shipped by Krupp, first to Buchenwald and then to Bergen-Belsen, but that Judith had become sick and had died the day after the British arrived. Uri's sobs awakened a large British nurse with a face like a bowl of fresh dough. As he was being pushed out of the tent, Uri heard Erika's hoarse voice call out a soft goodbye.

Some of the thousands of bodies found by the British at Bergen-Belsen.

Chapter 10

New Worlds

The sun was rising on the other side of the Elbe when Uri finished telling me what had happened to him after Auschwitz. His eyes were dry but mine weren't. I grieved for Judith, who had given up her chance to escape for Uri and had lost her life as a result. I was jealous of Erika because she had made love with Uri, but I grieved for her also after he told me she had died a few hours after he was made to leave her tent. And I was more completely in love with Uri than ever. Although school officials and most classmates were upset that I had spent almost the entire night talking with him, I was secretly pleased at their displeasure, confident that much of it stemmed from simple envy.

Uri and I continued to talk from time to time and sometimes took long walks along the river. I wanted to explore the picturesque village of Blankenese with him, but he remained very uncomfortable around Germans. At my urging he talked more about his experiences, filling in the details and answering my many questions. He told me that after he left Bergen-Belsen he headed toward Hungary but was arrested several times by the Russians, who wanted to subdue the roving bands of displaced persons whether they were former slaves or former SS. Advised by a friendly Russian officer that he would most likely be deported to the east if he returned home and tried to reclaim what had belonged to his family, he turned back west toward the address in France that his skeletal French friend had given him. But when he arrived, he learned that his friend's family had received no word from him since the end of the war and feared the worst. So Uri headed back to Essen to see if he could find the Frenchman.

He found that most of the slaves who had survived the Third Reich's death throes had fled the city a step or two behind their former guards. The new British and American masters of western Germany spoke English, chewed gum, and dashed around in Jeeps, seemingly oblivious of the monumental ruins and idle munitions workers all about them. After a few awkward attempts to find out what had happened to his friend, Uri joined a band of children, some of them former slaves and others simply orphans, who were staying alive by scavenging food at night from the garbage of an American officer's mess. Occasionally he found something he could trade or sell on the black market, but it was dangerous work because there was a guard posted at the dump who would sometimes shoot at the children or the rats that competed for the leftovers.

Eventually arrested and ticketed by the Red Cross for transport to Hungary, Uri told an American army sergeant who was Jewish and spoke German that he would almost certainly be deported to Russia if he was returned to his village. The sergeant didn't believe Uri at first, but took the trouble to look into the matter. As a result Uri remained in the area for more than a year, doing odd jobs for the Americans in return for food and tips. The sergeant also stopped the sniping at the garbage dump, which he said had not been authorized but had been carried out by a crazy but highly decorated soldier who was sorry the war had ended. When the sergeant received word that his unit would soon be returned to America, he contacted a Jewish relief agency and obtained a promise that they would arrange for

Uri to be given an opportunity to go to school. A few misadventures later, Uri was delivered to the school at Blankenese.

* * *

Creation of the state of Israel in May of 1948 was a cause for jubilation that shook the school to its foundation. The refugee organizations that had run the school as a way-station to Palestine were instantly eager to transfer the entire operation to the new state. Creation of a West German Republic one year later dissolved lingering support for a Hamburg campus. The generation that had been primarily responsible for the deaths of more than thirty million people was back in power after only a four-year hiatus, and, to no one's surprise, was happy to speed the departure of surviving Jews to Israel, where they would come under attack by Arab states. Because this meant Uri was going to Israel, I implored my father to let me go as well. But when a Zionist told me my mission would be to give birth to warriors, and to serve God, husband, and the new fatherland, the less enthusiastic I became. Father then surprised me by offering to adopt Uri. But Uri's heart was set on Israel, and I respected his choice. Heartbroken, I remained with my family.

Like the skies over Hamburg, the next several years were turbulent much of the time as our family was slowly torn apart by unresolved grief. For my mother, the loss of her mother, brother, aunt, and other relatives grew harder rather than easier to bear in the country of their murderers. Recklessly courageous and hopeful in the first postwar years, she grew increasingly discontented after the Allies abruptly turned on one another and reached for every asset they could lay hands on, including convicted criminals such as Alfried Krupp who had committed unspeakable atrocities.

Sometime after I began attending a Hamburg public school, where I was constantly hazed as the only Jew, I discovered that Mother had become attached to a woman whose oldest son had been a close friend of Mother's murdered younger brother, Hans. Liese Victor was not Jewish. She was an Aryan aristocrat—tall, blond, blue-eyed, the daughter of one of Hamburg's most popular public officials. She had been married to a Jew, a writer who had fled to Switzerland before the war and had chosen to live in East Germany after the war, leaving Liese and their two sons a second time. Father and I were grateful to Liese for offering a sympathetic shoulder to Mother, although I was not fond of her youngest son, whose nickname was Bully. Liese wanted her sons to emigrate to America and urged Mother to do the same. Miserable in Hamburg, I wholeheartedly concurred, taking it for granted that all or none of our family would go.

One Friday when I was fifteen I returned home from school early, having faked illness to avoid gym class, and discovered my mother and my father making love on the couch. After reentering through the back door and secretly confirming that what I had glimpsed was actually happening, I retreated to my room undetected, thrilled by what I had learned. I had always thought, or assumed without thinking about it, that sex was a nocturnal activity and that it required a bed. The fact that it could be enjoyed any time of the day or night and could be performed almost anywhere was thunderous news to me.

Possibly overstimulated by my newfound sophistication, I gave my parents a rather rude shock at a dinner party a few weeks later and even shocked myself as well. Toward the end of the dinner, Helmut Koeller, the artist who had helped Father to extract secrets from Nazi officials who sat for their portraits, asked me what I planned to do during the summer. I would soon be graduating from Hamburg's fine arts high school and, having decided to become an artist, I very much wanted him to take me as an apprentice in his atelier. Trying to give the impression that I was more sophisticated than I looked, I answered that "This summer I plan to have an affair."

All conversation stopped and Father looked at me as if he had never seen me before and didn't know what to make of my presence at the table. Aware that every eye was on me, I tried not to show

Me at age fifteen.

that I wished I had given any one of the other answers now scrolling through my head instead. Helmut Koeller didn't say anything but shifted his slightly puzzled look from my face to my mother's.

"That's perfectly understandable," Mother said. "Every young woman wants to have a love affair. I'm glad you've chosen to confide in us. Not many girls are so sensible, and end up bitterly disappointed. We can talk more about it later if you like."

"Listen to your mother," Father said hoarsely. "She can help you."

After all of the guests had departed, Mother came to my bedroom. "I admire your courage," Mother began. "I don't know anyone who is able to speak so candidly about having a love affair."

"I didn't mean to embarrass you in front of your friends," I said.

"Don't worry about it," she said. "Your Father is upset because he thinks you're much too young. But he's pleased that you aren't afraid to speak your mind. May I ask if your intended is someone we know?"

"No, you don't know him. That is, I haven't made up my mind yet."

"I understand," Mother said, "and you are right to consider carefully. It's one of the most important decisions any woman ever makes. Nothing else compares. It can lead to lasting happiness or to grief. It all depends on whether you pick a man who is sensitive and intelligent and understands you and how to care for you."

"How," I asked, "can you tell in advance whether he understands?"

"It's not always easy. But you can rule out boys or very young men. Even if they believe they love you, they lack the necessary experience. You must have a man of mature judgment who will be honest with you as well as loving. I think you are destined to have a great love, but only if you use your intelligence and are not impulsive."

After she had gone, I lay awake thinking about all the things she had said. Never before had she spoken to me in that way. I believed her. She was beautiful. Men adored her. She hadn't said no, just be sure to pick the right man. I had permission!

* * *

I was attending school in Switzerland when Mother moved in with Liese Victor and took Rena with her. When I returned to Hamburg and pleaded to be allowed to join her, Mother became distraught and retired to her bed. The next day Liese told me that Mother had a serious heart condition and that my talk about having an affair had given her a heart attack and nearly killed her. It was untrue, but I didn't learn that until years later. Terribly chastened and guilt-ridden, I vowed never to upset Mother again. When I visited her at Liese Victor's, I brought lots of flowers, looked my best and did all I could to make the visit a pleasant experience. On one of the last visits, however, Liese Victor looked me over and then remarked to Mother that I might look attractive if I didn't have such "*Neger-lippen.*"

My cheeks burning, I looked from Liese to my mother, who said nothing but smiled at Liese as if Liese had said something clever. For years I had been self-conscious about my lips, which were fuller and darker than those of Aryan girls. Nazi posters had depicted Jewish women as having garishly large mouths, and after the hate posters had been removed, students in postwar Hamburg had kept the racist message current by frequently calling me *Neger-lippen* and *Juden-lippen*. Liese was well aware of this. When the woman who had led me through the fires of war-torn Hamburg permitted Liese to say this to me, I was crushed by the realization that I had lost my mother's love.

The following autumn, again taking Rena with her, Mother departed for New York as the wife of Liese's youngest son, Bully. Everything about her leaving was so painful I couldn't see anything clearly. Father shushed any word of reproach, explaining that she had suffered too much loss at the hands of Germans to live among them. I understood this but not the need for divorce, a loveless remarriage, and separate custody, all of which were attributed to alleged immigration requirements. It took years to understand that the outrages that had compelled her to leave had compelled him to stay and fight.

Within a year, however, I persuaded him to let me go to New York, where I hoped to regain my mother's love. Almost immediately I fell in love with the city, and it seemed to fall for me. For the first time in my life, I felt safe. Nobody even seemed to know or care that I was a Jew. The people were possessed by an optimism and energy that would have seemed embarrassingly outré in Europe. But I couldn't get closer to Mother, because I couldn't stand living with Bully. He gave the impression of Teutonic self-control but was much too eager to help Rena and me to take a bath. I soon moved into a place of my own, a room in an elderly couple's Manhattan brownstone. Around a year later Bully landed a plum job in Los Angeles and moved there with Mother and Rena. I would have declined to go with them if asked, but Mother didn't ask. Some months later, Helga, who was still living with Father in Hamburg, managed to persuade Mother to let her join them in Los Angeles. When she stopped in New York to visit me, I noticed how Helga turned heads with her platinum hair, trim figure, and green-eyed enthusiasm for her new life.

Left completely on my own, I began to spend less time at Hunter College, where I was now enrolled, than dashing about in a Jeep as an unpaid assistant to a press photographer, getting close-up views of the action in diverse neighborhoods not usually visited by strangers. We even had a siren, which wasn't kosher but got us through traffic. At some point I discovered that fashion photographers were intrigued by my look and wanted me to model for them. This enabled me to pocket gobs of money and acquire designer clothes that undoubtedly helped me to land one of the best lowest-paying jobs in town on the staff of the cinema collection of the Museum of Modern Art. While there I met wonderful people, such as Eleanor Roosevelt, Greta Garbo, and the kind of man my

Almost seventeen and on my way to America.

mother had depicted—intelligent, sensitive, and caring—as worthy of a first *affaire d'amour*. I was twenty-one in 1957 when Daniel and I moved in together on Manhattan's Minetta Lane, never to part.

Two years earlier I had become alarmed and angered by the murder of Emmett Till, a fourteen-year-old African-American boy whose killers were set free by a white jury in Mississippi because he was said to have winked at a white woman. After that, and after my unsuccessful attempt to rent an apartment with an African-American girlfriend, I realized that racial discrimination was viewed as normal by many if not most Americans. I saw it as a variation on the persecution I had experienced in Europe. So did Daniel, who grew up, studied, and was licensed to practice law in the segregated South. When we moved to Washington, D.C., which was also highly segregated in 1960, we became active members of the Congress of Racial Equality, engaging in nonviolent direct action and civil disobedience to combat discrimination. I became a volunteer worker for the historic March on Washington in 1963 and a year later coordinated D.C. support for seating the integrated Mississippi Freedom Democrats at the National Convention in Atlantic City. Immediately after, at the invitation of civil rights heroine, Fannie Lou Hamer, I went to Mississippi as a field staff worker for the Student Nonviolent Coordinating Committee. When the Ku Klux Klan burned a cross in front of our Freedom School in Pascagoula, Mississippi, I painted **FREEDOM** on the charred crossbar and continued to teach.

Because of my experience with European racism, I had grown up with the firm belief that I had a duty to oppose racism wherever I found it. That was an article of faith in our family, but I had never been able to act on it effectively in Europe. So I not only welcomed it but was grateful for the opportunity in America to fight back against an evil that had taken so many lives and continued to injure countless more. One of the things that excited me the most about the American civil rights movement was the way it chose to fight—by confronting overwhelming power and terror with nonviolent resistance. Having seen what righteous as well as unrighteous warfare could do to people, I was opposed to violence except when absolutely necessary to save lives. And while not all who participated in the movement were equally committed to the principle of nonviolence, even those who would have preferred to fight fire with fire agreed to practice it regardless of the risks. For me, it was a privilege and often a joy to work with so many people with that kind of courage and conviction. And when, despite the murder of rights workers, bombings, beatings, assassinations, and incarcerations, we eventually won many of the rights we fought for nonviolently, I was no longer a victim; rather I was a combatant in a successful campaign against racial injustice. Nonviolent resistance had replaced the helpless rage I had felt as a child, and at the same time it had vindicated my painfully acquired belief in viable alternatives to the hands of war.

After I returned to Washington, Daniel enlisted in the War on Poverty, while I at one point was able to combine activism for civil rights, peace in Viet Nam, and women's liberation by working in the presidential campaign of African-American Congresswoman Shirley Chisholm. We were arrested separately on occasion and participated together in demonstrations aimed at South African apartheid. I took it personally when Ronald Reagan launched his presidential campaign in the Mississippi town where three civil rights workers had been murdered, to pledge his allegiance to "states' rights," the doctrine that had condoned segregation and shielded the murderers from punishment.

With the idealistic movements largely undone by rioting, backlash, political conniving, and their own historic successes, Daniel and I sold our modest house and moved to rural Tuscany where we lived in peace with fiercely independent hill villagers and enjoyed the splendors in nearby Rome, Florence, Siena, and Venice. While Daniel wrote the great American civil rights novel, I sketched and painted and made constructions with found objects that had once been useful. As I had begun to do in Washington after an astonishing variety of new yarns had rather suddenly become available in the 1970s, I also made colorful abstract fiber creations that could be worn or displayed as works of art. I experienced some modest success in exhibiting these works and placing them in collections and on the bodies of stylish people in cities across Europe and America. When we moved after a few years from Tuscany to the tiny Sicilian island of Levanzo, I continued to make wearable art, incorporating designs drawn, etched, and painted more than 10,000 years earlier on the walls of a cave there—prehistoric art that reminded me of the drawings I had made as a child in hiding.

After living for seven idyllic years on the island, and for several more years back in Tuscany, where we helped the same hill villagers celebrate the 300th anniversary of the abolition of the death penalty by the Archduke of Tuscany, we decided to move for a time to Hamburg. I wanted to talk with living relatives from my father's side of the family, including Cousin Inge, and learn more about our past. Both my parents were dead, but I knew I would be able to commune with my father's ghost at his gravesite in Hamburg's beautiful cemetery.

The memorial for those who died during Operation Gomorrah in the air-raid shelter of the Karstadt Department Store.

Chapter 11

The Children of Blankenese

As life itself proceeds from chance encounters, my rebirth in 2006 as one of the Children of Blankenese resulted from bumping into someone I barely knew, who invited me to join him for a cup of tea at Hamburg's Literature House. I accepted with pleasure because I greatly admired Peter Hesse for organizing the placement of small brass markers in sidewalks or streets fronting the last residences of Jews and Gypsies murdered by the Nazis. For many, including my grandmother, Rosa Singer, her son, Hans, and her sister-in-law, Emma, these four-by-four-inch plates, inscribed with the names, birth dates, years and places of the victims' murders, were their only memorial. Embedded in the sidewalks, the markers are called *stolpersteine*—or stumblestones.

At tea, overhearing Hesse's companions talking about an upcoming reunion of the schoolchildren of Blankenese, I mentioned that I had gone to school there after the war. I explained that it hadn't been a public school but rather a private retreat for the care of Jewish refugee children.

A stolpertstein *(memorial cobblestone) near the last residence of Great-Aunt Emma Muller.*

Stolpersteine *in front of the last residence of genocide victims.*

My husband, Daniel, beside the stolpersteine *for Grandmother Rosa and Uncle Hans Singer.*

"It was really wonderful," I said, "in a beautiful mansion overlooking the Elbe. But I don't think it's there anymore. I've looked for it several times and couldn't find it."

"It's still there," the two companions said, "and you're one of the Children of Blankenese!"

The women were members of a multidenominational Christian group in Blankenese that had taken an interest in the fate of Jews who had lived in their very picturesque and affluent community. After exhuming the shameful history of deportations to death camps, the group was glad to discover the story of the school on the Warburgs' estate—so glad that they organized a reunion for the first contingent of children given refuge, all of them orphans gleaned from the acres of corpses at the Bergen-Belsen concentration camp. It had been costly and difficult, since all the children had been shipped to Palestine, some on the Exodus, but so gratifying that they were now organizing a reunion of the second contingent, which included my sisters and me and I hoped would include Uri, my unruly first love.

I had been writing about Uri only weeks earlier, trying to recall details of his story about the murder of his family and his own incredible odyssey during the nightmare reign of the Nazis. The difficulty was that sixty years had passed and his story had been overlaid and intermingled with similar accounts of extraordinary suffering, most notably the bestial mistreatment of Jewish women exploited as slave laborers by arms magnate, Alfried Krupp. Their ordeal, documented in the record of the Krupp's war-crimes trial, had been related in William Manchester's magnificent history, *The Arms of Krupp*. Because my memory of Uri's story seemed to fit, and because I passionately believe that more people should know about this chapter in the history of war's depravity, I had written of Uri's sister as the woman, real but unidentified, who had turned back from what turned out to be a successful escape by other women. So far as I knew the reason one escapee had turned back had never been told, and I thought it might well have been in order to save another prisoner, possibly her brother. The school reunion, I hoped, would enable me to learn from Uri how far off the mark my surmise had been and to correct the account accordingly.

At dinner the first night, all of us were asked to tell how they had first come to Blankenese and what our thoughts about it were now. All but four or five were orphans from Hungary or Poland, retrieved by Zionist organizations from cloisters, woods, and cellars and taken secretly through eastern states and occupation zones to Blankenese. Each story was an improbable victory for life. One warm and very pleasant woman had been found as a baby without a name. No one even knew for certain when or where she had been born. At the school she had been given the Jewish name of Haya, which means life, and later smuggled into Palestine. Aside from not liking her name, which she thought was too old-fashioned, she was happy with her life in Israel and grateful to those at Blankenese who had nurtured her.

Extreme hunger was a dominant theme of the stories of these survivors, along with gratitude to the school not just for feeding them but for giving them their first experience of being with other children in a secure environment. One man said that before arriving at Blankenese he had assumed that constant hunger was the natural condition of life. He had been astounded when he was allowed to eat as much bread as he could hold. Living without parents in a world that wanted them dead, many of these children had done impossible things to survive. At an age when German children were not yet thinking of kindergarten, one boy had fled an overrun Polish ghetto and made his way alone across rivers and mountains to Kazakhstan and, still feeling unsafe, on to Tashkent at the eastern end of Uzbekistan.

The next day, after the group returned from a grim trip to Bergen-Belsen, I began to ask people if they had known Uri or anything about him, whether he was alive and, if so, where he might be now. I said that the last I had heard he was tending an orchard on a kibbutz somewhere. But no one knew anything. When asked why I was so interested, I explained that he was the first young man I wanted to be my young man. (After that several men in the group playfully insisted that their name was Uri.) To illustrate what a troubled youth Uri had been, I told how I had given him my watch as a present and he had immediately smashed it, saying that watches were tools of prison guards. One of the men then insisted that I take his Rolex. I declined, explaining that, because of Uri, I refused to wear one.

Each day I spent with the Children of Blankenese I became more enamored with the lot of them. They were the most immediately affectionate people I had ever met, affectionate to me, to my sisters, and to one another. They had defied fate by living and were determined to give life their best. Although several were shy, reserved, or more observant than engaging, we were a joyful bunch, laughing often, kissing and hugging all the time. Spontaneously or on request, feelings and opinions were freely shared. No one tried to be a star or insinuate that he or she was in any way more important than anyone else. Appreciation of the Germans who had brought us together was free flowing and richly deserved. Despite our gratitude, though, there was an unbridgeable gulf between the sponsors and the survivors. Having been denied a normal childhood, we were free to be as children together and feel the intense joy of finding forty-six brothers and sisters.

A sensitive subject for me was a question that was posed several times: Why had I never come to Israel? Even those who had lived in America believed that Israel was the only place where Jews could feel free to be Jews. Some who had lived in America for a time authoritatively affirmed that sentiment.

"You will all have to come when it happens again," one of them said, without having to explain what "it" meant, "and we will defend you."

The belief that Jews were threatened around the globe was broadly shared, as was their faith in fortress Israel. The speaker's voice had betrayed considerable bravado, however, and her expression after her prideful moment suggested that she still lived, as she had as a child, with fear.

When I responded that I was a confirmed pacifist who couldn't bite her tongue and would surely offend those who weren't part of the peace movement, they laughed and pooh-poohed the idea that I had anything to worry about. I was told repeatedly, "In Israel everyone speaks her own mind!"

By the time we parted, I had promised to go to Israel. Because my son and grandchildren were in America, I didn't want to live in Israel permanently. But I wanted to stay long enough to get to know my new brothers and sisters better, and to contribute if I could to a just peace. Many in my family had been murdered by racial hatred in the hands of war. Among the Children of Blankenese, I discovered the loving kinship I had lost as a child.

ILLUMINATIONS

A flare descending
And suddenly I see party balls
Like Christmas trees from books
Float through the sky enchanting me
And after flashing brilliant promises
Explode
I see them dancing still
Their magic becomes unbearable
Flame and thunder all around

Escaped one morning
Aged eight
No longer sentinel in war
But lying in a field of ripening grain
Upon a pillow of anemones
And their petaled reds upon my eyes
Shield me from the flames
Making dancers water-colored against the sky
Then through slanted downward gaze
I see my belly heave to heaven
And on cornflower splendored bed
I taste the sweet warm scent of peace
Taste life upon my lips
Kiss the smells
Listen to the music of the flowers
And forget

Acknowledgments

My father was the first to encourage me to write about my experience of war and genocide. He believed, and taught me to believe, that it was our duty to expose what had been done and do our best to discourage repetitions. My mother's courageous defiance of the Nazis also encouraged me to write this book. Because she could not bear to speak about what had been done to her and her family, I wanted to tell her story and theirs, so that they might be remembered and I might add my voice to those saying: NEVER AGAIN! But in New York in the late 1950s, when I tried to write about the fire-bombing of Hamburg in 1943, my mind would simply shut down. I was still too traumatized by that horror to revisit it. This changed the night my future husband Daniel held me in his arms while I retraced my flight with my mother through a city experiencing biblical destruction. Trembling and sobbing, I remembered what we wore and saw and encountered during Operation Gomorrah, including the charred bodies and the death agonies of people struck by white phosphorus. That night of near total recall not only removed my writer's block, it started me on a path of recovery and strength which I have happily shared with Daniel through more than fifty years. It is a gross understatement to say that without his help and support I would not have written this book.

I wish also to thank my wonderful and witty son, another Daniel, for his good-natured responses to hundreds of calls for help with my recalcitrant computer as I wrestled the manuscript into submission. Special thanks also to my sisters, Rena Victor and Helga Anderson, who shared the terror inflicted by the hands of war and supported my efforts to write about it. Both admiration and sincere appreciation are owed to Tony Lyons and his chief editor at Skyhorse, Jay Cassell, for selecting *The Hands of War* manuscript, and to editor, Holly Rubino, and the other capable staff members who transformed it into a book to be proud of. Warm thanks go to Andrew Clarke for sending Tony Lyons that manuscript.

Before the manuscript was much more than a single chapter, Ian Jack, then the already legendary editor of *Granta*, gave me the encouragement I needed to continue by telling me he was both moved and informed by my account of the bombing of Hamburg. He didn't have an issue about war in the works at the time, but a year later he did and he included *Operation Gomorrah*. Its reception far exceeded all my expectations—comparisons to John Hersey's *Hiroshima*, high praise in *The Manchester Guardian* and *The Irish Times*, and selection by famed writer David Foster Wallace and editor Robert Atwan for inclusion in *Best American Essays of 2007*. A portion of my family's vision of war had been broadly read and shared, reprinted even in Russia, and I shall be forever grateful.

I would be remiss if I failed to thank Justine Dymond, editor of *womenwriters.net* and Andrei Codrescu, editor of *Exquisite Corpse*, for their earlier enthusiasm for an abbreviated account of life in hiding. I also wish to thank Sergey and Kathy Shabutsky for shepherding the republication of *Operation Gomorrah* in the Russian literary journal *Inostrannaya Literatura*. I cannot close without expressing my warm appreciation to those who arranged for the reunion of the children who had been given refuge in a school at Blankenese and to those in Hamburg, Germany who placed brass *stolpersteine* in front of the last residence of family members deported and killed.

About the Author

Marione Ingram grew up in Hamburg, Germany, during World War II, the daughter of a Jewish mother and non-Jewish father. As well as the Holocaust, she experienced the firestorm bombings that killed tens of thousands of people and destroyed much of the city in 1943, and spent the last eighteen months of the war in hiding. In 1952 she moved to New York City, where she worked at the Museum of Modern Art and shared a studio with other aspiring artists. Moving to Washington, D.C., in 1960, she married, became a mother, a U.S. citizen, and a civil rights activist, and ran a Freedom School in Mississippi as a staff worker for the Student Nonviolent Coordinating Committee. She is a fiber artist whose works have been exhibited on both sides of the Atlantic and is currently writing a book about life on a small Sicilian island, on which she lived for seven years. She and her husband of more than fifty years, Daniel Ingram, currently live in Washington, D.C., to be near their son, also Daniel, and his wife Sally, and grandsons, Sam and Noah.